H. Richard Lamb, *University of Southern California*
EDITOR-IN-CHIEF

# Dual Diagnosis of Major Mental Illness and Substance Abuse Volume 2: Recent Research and Clinical Implications

Robert E. Drake
*Dartmouth Medical School*

Kim T. Mueser
*Dartmouth Medical School*

EDITORS

Number 70, Summer 1996

JOSSEY-BASS PUBLISHERS
San Francisco

DUAL DIAGNOSIS OF MAJOR MENTAL ILLNESS AND SUBSTANCE ABUSE
VOLUME 2: RECENT RESEARCH AND CLINICAL IMPLICATIONS
*Robert E. Drake, Kim T. Mueser* (eds.)
New Directions for Mental Health Services, no. 70
*H. Richard Lamb*, Editor-in-Chief

Microfilm copies of issues and articles are available in 16mm and 35mm, as well as microfiche in 105mm, through University Microfilms Inc., 300 North Zeeb Road, Ann Arbor, Michigan 48106-1346.

ISSN 0193-9416        ISBN 0-7879-9902-4

NEW DIRECTIONS FOR MENTAL HEALTH SERVICES is part of The Jossey-Bass Psychology Series and is published quarterly by Jossey-Bass Inc., Publishers, 350 Sansome Street, San Francisco, California 94104-1342.

EDITORIAL CORRESPONDENCE should be sent to the Editor-in-Chief, H. Richard Lamb, Department of Psychiatry and the Behavioral Sciences, U.S.C. School of Medicine, 1934 Hospital Place, Los Angeles, California 90033-1071.

Cover photograph by Wernher Krutein/PHOTOVAULT © 1990.

TCF  Manufactured in the United States of America on Lyons Falls Pathfinder Tradebook. This paper is acid-free and 100 percent totally chlorine-free.

# CONTENTS

# EDITORS' NOTES

Five years ago, when Kenneth Minkoff and Robert Drake edited the first volume of this title in this series, the field of dual diagnosis (defined here as co-occurring severe mental illness and substance use disorder) was just emerging. Awareness of the prevalence and complications of substance abuse and dependence in the population of persons with severe mental illness had been growing since the early 1980s, and clinicians and researchers were documenting the rates, presentations, and clinical features of dual diagnosis. More importantly, a general recognition was developing that the traditional separation between substance abuse programs and mental health programs in this country represented an impediment to serving patients with dual disorders. Clinicians and program managers were rapidly developing models of what has come to be called integrated treatment, that is, treatment in which the same programs and clinicians take responsibility for combining mental health and substance abuse interventions at the level of clinical service delivery rather than allowing the burden of coordinating two disparate treatment systems to fall on the patients themselves. The Minkoff and Drake volume was largely devoted to explicating the philosophy and emerging programmatic models of integrated dual-diagnosis treatment.

Since 1991 the movement toward providing integrated services has been embraced at all levels, and many research studies support the general effectiveness of integrated treatment. Available research now also addresses many aspects of services within integrated treatment programs. In other words, the field has moved from awareness and speculative service models to a data-based understanding of many aspects of dual-diagnosis treatment services. Programs today can and should be based on these research findings.

The chapters in this volume are intended to make current research findings comprehensible to all stakeholders in the system of care for people with dual disorders. Our goal is not just to summarize research on dual disorders but also to elucidate the clinical and services implications of the available research. Thus the book is intended to help planners, administrators, clinicians, other providers, families, and consumers who are in the process of advocating, developing, implementing, and participating in effective programs.

Chapters in this volume specifically address several aspects of dual diagnosis: the difficulties and current guidelines for assessment, general dual-diagnosis treatment guidelines, group interventions for dual disorders, housing for persons with dual diagnosis, the relationships between dual diagnosis and families, the costs of dual-diagnosis treatment, and the rates and patterns of substance abuse and dependence in persons with severe mental disorders. The more clinically oriented chapters in the first half of the volume include vignettes to illustrate the chapters' contents.

The dual-diagnosis research community is a small one and is well represented in this volume. Contributors were asked to summarize not only their own research but also the work of others in their specific areas. We extend our appreciation to all of them for diligently fulfilling this task.

Robert E. Drake
Kim T. Mueser
Editors

ROBERT E. DRAKE, M.D., Ph.D., is professor of psychiatry and community and family medicine at Dartmouth Medical School and director of the New Hampshire–Dartmouth Psychiatric Research Center.

KIM T. MUESER, Ph.D., is associate professor of psychiatry and community and family medicine at Dartmouth Medical School and a senior researcher at the New Hampshire–Dartmouth Psychiatric Research Center.

*Assessment of dually diagnosed patients consists of three steps:
detection, diagnosis, and specialized assessment for treatment
planning. Each of these is informed by recent research.*

# Assessing Substance Use Disorder in Persons with Severe Mental Illness

*Robert E. Drake, Stanley D. Rosenberg, Kim T. Mueser*

## Case Study: John D

A lawyer called the mental health center about a twenty-seven-year-old homeless man, John D, who had been arrested several times after threatening women in public. John, who was disheveled, paranoid, and verbally abusive, explained to an outreach case manager that the FBI was following him and directing women on the streets to control his thoughts. This problem had been worsening for three or four years. John had been hospitalized and given medications involuntarily on several occasions. He denied using alcohol or other drugs. Hospital records, obtained subsequently, corroborated this history, including the lack of alcohol and drug problems.

The outreach case manager began to meet John each morning for coffee and helped him to secure entitlements and housing. After several weeks of building a relationship, John agreed to take a small dose of medicine to alleviate his problems with sleep, anxiety, and fears. Nevertheless, his psychosis and public invective flared up periodically and he continued to have difficulties with the police. During another hospitalization precipitated by further threats, a urine drug test revealed high levels of cannabis. John then admitted to his case manager a pattern of heavy cannabis use over several years. The treatment plan changed as John and his case manager began to explore the role of marijuana in his life and in his course of illness. He suffered from delusions, hallucinations, and paranoia even when he was not using cannabis, and his symptoms became much worse and led to threatening behavior when he was using cannabis heavily. He was given two diagnoses—schizophrenia and cannabis use disorder.

After several months of exploring the nature of his substance abuse, John and his case manager had identified six risk factors that led to cannabis use:

feeling anxious around people, eating at the soup kitchen where cannabis was sold and traded, hanging around with other homeless persons who used cannabis daily, boredom, not having a safe place to sleep, and getting angry with his parents. Next, they developed a treatment plan that both addressed each of these problems with specific behavioral strategies and provided further drug education and treatment. John's cannabis use gradually decreased and stopped over the course of ten months.

## Substance Abuse Assessment

Over the past decade awareness of substance abuse and dependence in persons with severe mental illness has grown steadily (Lehman and Dixon, 1995; Minkoff and Drake, 1991; Ridgely, Osher, and Talbott, 1987). Despite this awareness and the costly consequences of nondetection (Kofoed, 1991; Lehman, Myers, and Corty, 1989), substance disorders are still underdiagnosed in this population (Ananth and others, 1989; Drake and others, 1990). Nondetection is attributable to a variety of factors, some generic to the problem of asking people to disclose their own socially proscribed behavior, and some specific to the complications of substance abuse diagnoses in persons with psychiatric illness. Concealing substance use patterns is very common in our culture; additional problems related to communication, memory, attitudes, and perception arise when assessing persons with severe mental illness. More valid, practical procedures have been developed, but assessment is still complicated by the technical limitations of available procedures and by the complex overlaps and interactions between severe mental illness and psychoactive substance use. In this chapter we review issues related to assessing substance use disorders in severely mentally ill patients, provide information from recent research, and discuss current procedures and new research directions.

## Scope of Problem

In this review, we will discuss three primary functions of assessment: detection, diagnosis, and specialized assessment for treatment planning. *Detection* refers to procedures for identifying substance dependence, substance abuse, or harmful or dangerous use that does not qualify for a diagnosis (Babor, Kranzler, and Lauerman, 1989). The *diagnostic* term "substance use disorder" refers to a habitual pattern of alcohol use or other drug use that results in significant impairments in areas of adjustment (American Psychiatric Association, 1987; 1994). Use disorders are divided into two mutually exclusive classifications—*substance abuse* and *substance dependence*—with the latter characterized by greater severity, physiological dependence, and compulsive use. *Specialized assessment* involves measuring the severity of the substance-related problems, the client's motivation and participation in treatment, and the conditions associated with the occurrence of problematic use that become targets for treatment interventions (Drake and Mercer-McFadden, 1995). Before discussing these three aspects of assessment, we briefly review research on prevalence and the problem of nondetection.

**Prevalence.** Substance use disorder is the most common comorbid complication among severely mentally ill persons (Minkoff and Drake, 1991). The Epidemiological Catchment Area (ECA) study (Regier and others, 1990) found that all persons with psychiatric disorders were more prone to substance disorder than the general population, but those with severe mental illness were especially vulnerable, with lifetime prevalence of approximately 50 percent. For example, persons with schizophrenia were more than four times as likely to have had a substance use disorder during their lifetimes and those with bipolar disorder were more than five times as likely to have such a diagnosis than persons in the general population. The evidence that persons with severe mental disorders are at increased risk for substance use disorders is reviewed in this volume by Cuffel.

**Nondetection.** Many studies show that substance disorders are underdetected and underdiagnosed in acute-care psychiatric settings, with rates of nondetection as high as 98 percent (Ananth and others, 1989). Failure to detect substance abuse disorder results in misdiagnosis of the psychiatric disorder, suboptimal pharmacological treatment of psychiatric syndromes, neglect of appropriate interventions for substance abuse (such as detoxification, education, and counseling), and inappropriate treatment planning and referral (Crowley, Chesluk, Dilts, and Hart, 1974; Kofoed, 1991; Lehman, Myers, and Corty, 1989).

The underdetection of comorbid substance disorders in psychiatric settings is caused by a combination of factors (Drake and others, 1990; Magliozzi, Kanter, Csernansky, and Hollister, 1983; Safer, 1987; Test, Wallisch, Allness, and Ripp, 1989), including clinicians' lack of awareness of the high rates of substance disorders in psychiatric populations; clinicians' inattention to substance abuse as a problem; the inadequacy of standard assessment instruments in this population; psychiatric patients' denial, minimization, and failure to see the relation between their substance use and problems of adjustment; and patients' cognitive, psychotic, and other impairments related to their psychiatric illness.

## Detection Procedures

To overcome the problem of invalid assessment of substance disorder in psychiatric patients, clinicians and researchers have recommended using multiple instruments, multiple perspectives, or multiple modes of assessment (Blankertz and Cnaan, 1994; Corse, Hirschinger, and Zanis, 1995; Drake, Alterman, and Rosenberg, 1993; Drake and Mercer-McFadden, 1995; Goldfinger and others, in press; Kofoed, 1991; Safer, 1987). Studies that have included these procedures have demonstrated greater sensitivity to detection (Drake and others, 1990; Galletely, Field, and Prior, 1993; Goldfinger and others, in press; Shaner and others, 1993; Stone, Greenstein, Gamble, and McLellan, 1993; Test, Wallisch, Allness, and Ripp, 1989). Ideally, substance abuse screening should incorporate an awareness of base rates and clinical and behavioral correlates, a self-report instrument designed specifically for persons with severe mental illness, and concurrent procedures to circumvent the problem of unreliable and invalid self-reports. Additional procedures that have proved useful in detecting substance abuse in other settings are laboratory evaluations, collateral reports, and physical signs and symptoms. Many of these procedures have not been carefully studied in psychiatric patients.

**Index of Suspicion.** Because co-occurring substance disorder is the most common complicating feature of severe psychiatric illness, mental health clinicians need to develop and maintain assessment skills and a high index of suspicion, especially when demographic features or other aspects of the patient's presentation suggest substance disorder. For example, although substance disorder affects approximately half of all patients with severe mental illness, it is even more common among young males (Cuffel, this volume; Drake, Osher, and Wallach, 1989; Mueser, Yarnold, and Bellack, 1992). The correlates of alcohol and drug abuse that increase risk status in this population include younger age, male gender, family history of substance abuse, homelessness, disruptive behavior, poor relationships with family, repeated hospitalizations, legal difficulties, and incarceration (Alterman and Erdlen, 1983; Alterman, Erdlen, McLellan, and Mann, 1980; Drake, Osher, and Wallach, 1989; Haywood and others, 1995; Mueser, Yarnold, and Bellack, 1992; Negrete and Knapp, 1986; Noordsy, Drake, Biesanz, and McHugo, 1994; Richard, Liskow, and Perry, 1985; Yesavage and Zarcone, 1983).

**Self-Report.** Assessment usually begins with direct interview, and a number of studies have shown that structured interviews yield valuable information that is reliable and specific but not necessarily sensitive (Drake and others, 1990; Goldfinger and others, in press). Self-report is less sensitive for detecting illicit drugs (Galletely, Field, and Prior, 1993; Shaner and others, 1993; Stone, Greenstein, Gamble, and McLellan, 1993) and should therefore be supplemented by collateral information or laboratory assessments (Drake, Alterman, and Rosenberg, 1993).

Standard interview instruments have several limitations with this population. For example, lengthy interviews are not practical in many treatment settings (Barbee and others, 1989), and standard instruments often assess consequences that are inappropriate or irrelevant for psychiatric patients (Corse, Hirschinger, and Zanis, 1995). If interview is the only means of assessment available, combining more than one instrument has been found useful (Drake and others, 1990; Goldfinger and others, in press).

We currently use the following procedures for direct interview: First, screen for lifetime difficulties by using, for example, the screening portion of the Structured Clinical Interview DSM-IV-R (Spitzer, Williams, Gibbon, and First, 1988). Second, use a calendar method to document use patterns in recent months (Sobell and others, 1980). Third, if there is any evidence of use of alcohol or other drugs, use a brief checklist such as the MAST (Selzer, 1971) or DAST (Skinner, 1982) to assess consequences. Supplement the MAST or DAST by asking about problems that are more common in psychiatric illness, such as homelessness, legal problems, and exacerbation of psychiatric disorder. Fourth, assess moderate alcohol use, which may have adverse consequences or portend future problems for this population (Drake, Osher, and Wallach, 1989; Drake and Wallach, 1993); recent, regular use, which may offer a better indicator of need for treatment than abuse (Dixon and others, 1993); and past history, which often provides a sensitive indicator of current problems (Barry and others, 1995). Finally, when conducting interviews, employ several general procedures that increase the validity of self-reported information: If possible, use self-report instruments when the client is stabilized; in the context of a careful, nonjudgmental, clinical interview that enables the client to relax and assures confidentiality; and in conjunction with laboratory assessment. Repeat self-report assessments on a regular basis (Babor, Stephen, and Marlatt, 1987).

**Collateral Sources.** People who know the client well can often provide accurate information about substance use and adverse consequences. Several studies have shown that clinicians are able to monitor substance use among psychiatric patients (Drake and others, 1990; Drake, Osher, and Wallach, 1989; Goldfinger and others, in press; Barry and others, 1995; Mueser and others, 1995; Test, Wallisch, Allness, and Ripp, 1989). Case managers, for example, can easily be trained to assess substance use and consequences according to standard criteria, and we have developed scales and rating forms—the Alcohol Use Scale and the Drug Use Scale—for this purpose (Drake, Mueser, and McHugo, 1996). When available, close personal contacts such as family members, friends, and housemates can help the clinical case manager with screening and monitoring (Osher and Kofoed, 1989; Ryglewicz, 1991). Patients with severe mental illness, however, often have constricted social networks and live in isolated settings so that collaterals are unavailable. In addition, because illicit drug use is often secretive, collateral informants may be more aware of alcohol use than of illicit drug use.

**Laboratory Tests.** Clinical investigators often recommend routine urine drug screening for all incoming psychiatric patients (Safer, 1987). Several studies have used urine drug tests to detect high rates of unreported illicit substance use in this population (Blumberg, Cohen, Heaton, and Klein, 1971; Galletely, Field, and Prior, 1993; Shaner and others, 1993; Stone, Greenstein, Gamble, and McLellan, 1993). Moreover, using laboratory tests is likely to increase the accuracy of clients' self-reports (Stone, Greenstein, Gamble, and McLellan, 1993).

The obvious shortcoming of urine drug tests is that they provide a limited indication of the frequency and amount of use and yield no information about the consequences of use. Some indirect information on frequency and amount can be obtained through repeated tests, and even one positive test serves to include substance abuse in the differential diagnosis. Clinicians should also be aware of issues related to sensitivity, quality control, and detection interval after use with specific tests, laboratories, and drugs (Gold and Dackis, 1986).

Blood chemistries and Breathalyzers are not as satisfactory for the detection of alcohol use as urine drug testing is for illicit drug use. Blood tests such as liver enzymes and red blood cell morphology are primarily sensitive to heavy alcohol use in the past three to six weeks (Babor, Kranzler, and Lauerman, 1989) and have only moderate sensitivity for detecting heavy drinking in psychiatric patients (Toland and Moss, 1989). Breathalyzer assessments are limited by the short time window (several hours or less), the high initial investment for equipment, the need for frequent recalibration, and a high need for technician support. We instead use a simple, inexpensive saliva test to detect the presence of alcohol (Cox and Crifasi, 1990).

**Other Procedures.** Other procedures for detecting substance use have not been tested in psychiatric patients. Procedures that deserve study include medical history and examination (Skinner, Holt, Sheu, and Israel, 1986), questions regarding traumatic injuries and clinical signs (Babor, DeLaFuente, Saunders, and Grant, 1989), and historical indicators such as childhood conduct disorder (Babor, DeLaFuente, Saunders, and Grant, 1989).

Table 1.1 lists currently used procedures for detection and diagnosis.

## Diagnosis

Making the diagnosis of substance use disorder in persons with severe mental illness is complicated in several ways. The specific criteria and thresholds for diagnosis have not been validated in patients with severe psychiatric illness and may need clarification. Evidence for a reconsideration of criteria and thresholds includes the following: These patients may be especially vulnerable to small amounts of substances (Knudsen and Vilmar, 1984; Drake, Osher, and Wallach, 1989; Lieberman, Kinon, and Loebel, 1990). They appear to have less severe substance disorders than primary substance abusers according to traditional criteria (Lehman, Myers, Corty, and Thompson, 1994), but they often experience adverse effects that are different from those experienced by primary substance abusers (Corse, Hirschinger, and Zanis, 1995). Finally, the physiological dependence syndrome may be less significant in patients with severe mental illness than in other substance abusers (Drake and others, 1990).

Although considered a residual category in DSM-III-R, substance abuse (as opposed to dependence) is actually quite common in persons with severe mental illness (Drake and others, 1990). Furthermore, the abuse versus dependence distinction may be etiologically important and prognostically useful in the population of severely ill psychiatric patients. Those with abuse rather than dependence are less likely to have family histories of substance disorder (Noordsy, Drake, Biesanz, and McHugo, 1994) and appear to have a better long-term prognosis, which suggests the possibility of different treatment needs (Bartels, Drake, and Wallach, 1995).

The current DSM-IV definition of abuse (American Psychiatric Association, 1994) involves a maladaptive pattern of use leading to adverse conse-

### Table 1.1.  Techniques for Identifying Alcohol and Illicit Drug Use

| Technique | Advantages | Disadvantages |
| --- | --- | --- |
| Lab tests | • Increases accuracy of self-report.<br>• Adds sensitivity when patients are defensive or cognitively impaired. | • Limited indication of frequency and amount of use.<br>• Temporal range very limited. |
| Self-report | Data on both current and lifetime use. Patients may be more willing to admit to alcohol use than drug use. | • Poor validity when there are reasons to deny or minimize substance use.<br>• Interviews not always feasible in acute treatment settings. Patients may be defensive or cognitively impaired. |
| Physical signs and symptoms | Case managers are capable of making longitudinal observations that are quite sensitive to alcohol use, and are sensitive to the changes that accompany drug abuse. | • Sensitivity of physical exam and medical history not tested in this population.<br>• Several signs and symptoms overlap with psychotic and agitated states. |
| Collateral sources | • Collaterals may be more aware of alcohol use than illicit drug use.<br>• When available, close personal contacts can help with screening and monitoring. | • Many severely mentally ill persons do not have collaterals.<br>• Collaterals typically have incomplete information. |
| Sociodemographic and other correlates | Age, gender, and clinical correlates can be used to identify high-risk patients. | Relatively little data on this specific population. |
| Indirect measures | May increase sensitivity when patients are defensive or cognitively impaired. | Not yet fully developed. |

quences in the absence of dependence. Recurrent exacerbation of psychological problems, however, which was a sufficient criterion for an abuse diagnosis in DSM-III-R, has been omitted from DSM-IV—a change that may be particularly significant for dually diagnosed persons, because the maladaptive nature of their use often involves interaction with mental illness. How these and other changes from DSM-III-R to DSM-IV will affect classification of persons with severe mental illness remains to be studied. National survey data suggest that in the general population the DSM-IV diagnosis of substance abuse without dependence will be far less prevalent (.06 percent) than was the DSM-III-R diagnosis (2.38 percent) (Grant, 1992).

The issue of diagnostic heterogeneity and its possible role in matching patients with treatments is poorly understood. Using latent class analysis, Cuffel, Heithoff, and Lawson (1993) identified two groups of dually diagnosed schizophrenic patients: alcohol or marijuana abusers and multiple-drug abusers. This diagnostic difference may have implications for treatment; it was later found to be important in predicting community violence, with multiple-drug abusers exhibiting higher levels of violence (Cuffel, Shumway, Chouljian, and MacDonald, 1994).

Although this chapter focuses on assessing substance use, the co-occurring psychiatric diagnosis is equally important in determining heterogeneity. Substance disorder comorbidity clearly affects diagnostic validity and makes differential diagnosis very difficult in some cases (Lehman, Myers, and Corty, 1989). Patients with psychiatric syndromes that are induced by substance disorder probably have different treatment needs from those who have two independent, co-occurring disorders (Lehman, Myers, Thompson, and Corty, 1993). Diagnostic heterogeneity within the dual-disorder population undoubtedly has further implications for treatment. For example, research indicates that patients with severe and persistent affective disorders, as opposed to psychotic disorders, are more socially competent and more able to participate in groups that require higher functioning, including self-help groups (Noordsy, Schwab, Fox, and Drake, 1996).

## Specialized Assessment

Once substance use disorders have been detected and diagnosed, the transition to treatment planning requires more detailed, individual information. Specialized assessment yields specific information for planning treatment by exploring three areas: the nature and severity of the problematic substance-using behaviors, the stage of treatment, and the factors associated with the maintenance of the problematic substance-using behaviors.

**Nature and Severity of Substance-Using Behaviors.** Substance-using behaviors should first be thoroughly described, including time, duration, frequency, level of intensity, and quantity of use; severity; developmental use history; physiological, cognitive, behavioral, and environmental systems involved in the behaviors; and the immediate and delayed consequences of use (Donovan, 1988). Physiological factors include tolerance, dependence, and withdrawal, as well as the medical sequelae of substance use. Cognitive factors include positive and negative expectancies related to use, such as enhanced mood, improved social ease, or enhanced feelings of arousal. Behavioral factors include interpersonal coping strategies and communication skills. Environmental factors include the social context of use, such as peer pressure. Although a number of instruments are available, no standardized measures for assessing the nature and severity of substance disorder have been validated in dual-disorder patients.

Assessment should investigate all relevant domains but should be individualized and should correspond to the duration of the substance-using behavior. For example, extensive neuropsychological testing may not be important for the young, moderate drinker, but is often critical for an older person with a long drinking history (Donovan, Kivlahan, Walker, and Umlauf, 1985).

Severity of psychiatric symptoms and response to antipsychotic medications may also be important dimensions. Our clinical experience suggests that persistent psychosis often renders substance abuse treatment ineffective, and case studies indicate that a positive response to clozapine is associated with reduced substance use (Marcus and Snyder, 1995).

**Stage of Treatment.** One central aspect of assessment is the individual's stage of change and stage of treatment. Prochaska, DiClemente, and Norcross (1992) have found that individuals with substance use disorder change in a predictable sequence, whether they do so on their own or in relation to a treatment program. Although assessing this process might have implications for treatment, there are currently no studies of this scheme in psychiatric patients.

Osher and Kofoed (1989) independently derived a similar model for the stage of treatment, which focuses less on internal motivational states and more on the client's level of behavioral involvement in substance abuse treatment. A client in the *engagement* stage develops a trusting relationship with treatment staff. During *persuasion,* clients learn more about the role that alcohol and drugs have played in their lives and develop motivation for change. They use specific strategies and interventions during *active treatment* to reduce their substance use. When these gains are stable, other specific strategies are employed as part of *relapse prevention.* Our group operationalized these stages of recovery in order to create a psychometrically sound scale to determine stage of treatment: the Substance Abuse Treatment Scale (SATS), which can be used reliably by clinicians or researchers (McHugo, Drake, Burton, and Ackerson, 1995).

The SATS helps clinicians determine the range of interventions that might be effective in relation to the client's current level of motivation and behavioral change (Drake and Noordsy, 1994). Thus the most immediate goal when working with a client in the engagement phase is to establish a helping relationship, or *treatment alliance.* Efforts to convince clients to address their substance abuse before such a relationship is established are usually premature and may drive clients away from treatment. In the persuasion phase, several strategies may enable the client to perceive the relationship between substance use and problems in living (see Carey's chapter in this volume). During active treatment, clients may make use of different interventions to modify risk factors such as lack of employment, a substance-abusing peer network, and craving. It should be noted that the efficacy of specific interventions and of the stagewise concept of treatment needs to be studied in depth.

**Conditions Associated with Abuse.** Substance abuse is currently viewed as a complex biopsychosocial disorder in which genetic, biological, psychological, cognitive, social, and environmental factors combine to predispose an individual to disorder; another combination of potentially overlapping factors sustains the disorder (Donovan, 1988). Thus, for example, for a particular individual with schizophrenia, factors such as family history of alcoholism, social anxiety, expectancies of decreased anxiety and increased social friendships, boredom, hopelessness, lack of activities, and living with substance-abusing peers may all contribute to a drug disorder. The essence of treatment planning is to identify these specific factors as targets of intervention. This approach underlies cognitive (Beck, Wright, Newman, and Liese, 1993) and behavioral (Monti, Abrams, Kadden, and Cooney, 1989) approaches to substance abuse treatment. As an example, for the patient described above the treatment team might consider some combination of the following interventions: a multiple-family group to address family issues, social skills training to overcome social anxiety without alcohol, cognitive therapy to modify expectancies, participation in a supported employment program to combat boredom and inactivity, and modification of the subject's living situation. Typically, not all of these can be changed at once, which is why recovery tends to take place over months and years rather than weeks (Drake, Mueser, Clark, and Wallach, 1996).

Recent evidence indicates that one important risk factor for substance abuse—trauma history—has often been ignored in treatment. Research shows that a high proportion of patients with severe mental illness have evidence of recent and past sexual and physical trauma, and that trauma history is associated with substance disorder (Goodman, Dutton, and Harris, 1995; Rosenberg, Drake, and Mueser, in press). Anecdotally, trauma history is identified as critical by clinicians in almost every dual-diagnosis program that we have visited. Clinicians are beginning to develop interventions that focus specifically on the poor self-care and self-destructive behaviors associated with trauma history in dually diagnosed persons (Harris, in press). Although no outcome data are yet available, we expect that this will be an important line of research in coming years.

Only limited evidence supports the efficacy of the type of individualized assessment and treatment planning discussed in this section. Two recent quasi-experimental studies show that the specific types of cognitive-behavioral and social networking interventions that are implied by this approach are effective with dually diagnosed individuals (Drake and others, 1996; Jerrell and Ridgely, 1995). In each study specific, individualized interventions with a focus on cognitive, behavioral, and social network factors produced better outcomes than other treatments.

## Future Research

There is a great need to develop substance use assessment instruments that are specifically tailored for persons with severe mental illness. Ideally such instruments should address the utility of multimodal procedures and should also address the three phases of screening, diagnostic assessment, and specialized assessment. Our group is now engaged in developing optimal screening and diagnostic instruments based on available interviews, questionnaires, laboratory procedures, collateral interviews, and indirect measures. By administering these assessment procedures to a large sample of severely mentally ill patients, we are working to develop a brief screening instrument for identifying substance-abusing patients in acute-care psychiatric settings. We are also working to develop a multimodal, diagnostic procedure for alcohol, cannabis, and cocaine abuse and dependence in persons with severe mental illness. This latter procedure is being designed for acute situations in which time, patient cooperation, and other resources allow a more extensive assessment. In addition to these studies, the field needs comprehensive instruments specific to persons with severe mental illness that assess the nature and severity of substance disorder and the specific factors that are associated with the substance-using behaviors.

## Conclusion

Severely ill psychiatric patients constitute an extremely vulnerable, high-risk group for substance abuse and dependence. They should therefore receive routine screening in all treatment programs. Currently, substance abuse is frequently underdetected in acute-care psychiatric settings. A few simple procedures could improve current rates of detection dramatically. Mental health professionals assessing in acute-care settings need to be educated about the high rates of substance abuse among severely mentally ill persons, the common correlates of substance abuse, basic detection techniques, and the importance of accurate diagnosis for appropriate treatment.

Some progress has been made in terms of understanding the limits of instruments currently used for primary substance abusers. More work is needed to develop and refine screening instruments and procedures to detect and diagnose alcohol- and drug-related problems in severely mentally ill persons. In addition, the development of instruments that enable clinicians to go from diagnosis to treatment planning should be a priority for researchers.

## References

Alterman, A. I., and Erdlen, D. L. "Illicit Substance Use in Hospitalized Psychiatric Patients: Clinical Observations." *Journal of Psychiatric Research and Evaluation*, 1983, 5, 377–380.

Alterman, A. I., Erdlen, F. R., McLellan, A. T., and Mann, S. C. "Problem Drinking in Hospitalized Schizophrenic Patients." *Addictive Behaviors*, 1980, 5, 273–276.

American Psychiatric Association. *Diagnostic and Statistical Manual of Mental Disorders* (3rd ed., revised). Washington, D.C.: American Psychiatric Press, 1987.

American Psychiatric Association. *Diagnostic and Statistical Manual of Mental Disorders* (4th ed.). Washington, D.C.: American Psychiatric Press, 1994.

Ananth, J., Vandewater, S., Kamal, M., Broksky, A., Gamal, R., and Miller, M. "Missed Diagnosis of Substance Abuse in Psychiatric Patients." *Hospital and Community Psychiatry*, 1989, 4, 297–299.

Babor, T. F., DeLaFuente, J. R., Saunders, J., and Grant, M. *AUDIT: The Alcohol Use Disorders Identification Test, Guidelines for Use in Primary Health Care*. Geneva, Switzerland: World Health Organization, 1989.

Babor, T. F., Kranzler, H. R., and Lauerman, R. J. "Early Detection of Harmful Alcohol Consumption: Comparison of Clinical, Laboratory, and Self-Report Screening Procedures." *Addictive Behaviors*, 1989, *14*, 139–157.

Babor, T. F., Stephen, R. S., and Marlatt, G. A. "Verbal Report Methods in Clinical Research on Alcoholism: Response Bias and its Minimization." *Journal of Studies on Alcohol*, 1987, *48*, 410–424.

Barbee, J. G., Clark, P. D., Crapanzano, M. S., Heintz, G. C., and Kehoe, C. E. "Alcohol and Substance Abuse Among Schizophrenic Patients Presenting to an Emergency Psychiatric Service." *Journal of Nervous and Mental Disease*, 1989, *177*, 400–407.

Barry, K. L, Fleming, M. F., Greenley, J., Widlak, P., Kropp, S., and McKee, D. "Assessment of Alcohol and Other Drug Disorders in the Seriously Mentally Ill." *Schizophrenia Bulletin*, 1995, *21*, 315–321.

Bartels, S. J., Drake, R. E., and Wallach, M. A. "Long-Term Course of Substance Use Disorders in Severe Mental Illness." *Psychiatric Services*, 1995, *46*, 248–251.

Beck, A. T, Wright, P. D., Newman, C. F., and Liese, B. S. *Cognitive Therapy of Substance Abuse*. New York: Guilford Press, 1993.

Blankertz, L. E., and Cnaan, R. A. "Assessing the Impact of Two Residential Programs for Dually Diagnosed Homeless Individuals." *Social Services Review*, 1994, *68*, 536–560.

Blumberg, A. G., Cohen, M., Heaton, A. M., and Klein, D. F. "Covert Drug Abuse Among Voluntary Hospitalized Psychiatric Patients." *Journal of the American Medical Association*, 1971, *217*, 1659–1661.

Corse, S. J., Hirschinger, N. B., and Zanis, D. "The Use of the Addiction Severity Index with Persons with Severe Mental Illness Face Validity." *Psychiatric Rehabilitation Journal*, 1995, *19* (1), 9–18.

Cox, R. A., and Crifasi, J. A. "A Comparison of a Commercial Microdiffusion Method and Gas Chromatography for Ethanol Analysis." *Journal of Analytic Toxicology*, 1990, *14*, 211–212.

Crowley, T. J., Chesluk, D., Dilts, S., and Hart, R. "Drug and Alcohol Abuse Among Psychiatric Admissions." *Archives of General Psychiatry*, 1974, *30*, 13–20.

Cuffel, B., Heithoff, K. A., and Lawson, W. "Correlates of Patterns of Substance Abuse Among Patients with Schizophrenia." *Hospital and Community Psychiatry*, 1993, *44*, 247–251.

Cuffel, B., Shumway, M., Chouljian, T. L., and MacDonald, T. "A Longitudinal Study of Substance Use and Community Violence in Schizophrenia." *Journal of Nervous and Mental Disease*, 1994, *182*, 704–708.

Dixon, L., Dibietz, E., Myers, P., Conley, R., Medoff, D., and Lehman, A. F. "Comparison of DSM-III-R Diagnoses and a Brief Interview for Substance Use Among State Hospital Patients." *Hospital and Community Psychiatry*, 1993, *44*, 748–752.

Donovan, D. M. "Assessment of Addictive Behaviors: Implications of an Emerging Biopsychosocial Model." In D. M. Donovan and G. A. Marlatt (eds.), *Assessment of Addictive Behavior*. New York: Guilford Press, 1988, 3–48.

Donovan, D. M., Kivlahan, D. R., Walker, R. D., and Umlauf, R. "Derivation and Validation of Neuropsychological Clusters Among Male Alcoholics." *Journal of Studies on Alcohol*, 1985, *46*, 205–211.

Drake, R. E., Alterman, A. I., and Rosenberg, S. D. "Detection of Substance Use Disorders in Severely Mentally Ill Patients." *Community Mental Health Journal*, 1993, *29*, 175–192.

Drake, R. E., and Mercer-McFadden, C. "Assessment of Substance Abuse Among Persons with Severe Mental Disorders." In A. F. Lehman and L. Dixon (eds.), *Double Jeopardy: Chronic Mental Illness and Substance Abuse*. New York: Harwood Academic Press, 1995, 47–62.

Drake, R. E., Mueser, K. T., Clark, R. E., and Wallach, M. A. "The Natural History of Substance Use Disorder in Persons with Severe Mental Illness." *American Journal of Orthopsychiatry*, 1996, *66*, 42–51.

Drake, R. E., Mueser, K. T., and McHugo, G. J. "Using Clinician Rating Scales to Assess Substance Abuse Among Persons with Severe Mental Disorders." In L. I. Sederer and B. Dickey (eds.), *Outcomes Assessment in Clinical Practice.* Baltimore: Williams and Wilkins, 1996, 113–116.

Drake, R. E., and Noordsy, D. L. "Case Management for People with Coexisting Severe Mental Disorder and Substance Use Disorder." *Psychiatric Annals,* 1994, *24,* 27–31.

Drake, R. E., Osher, F. C., Noordsy, D. L., Hurlbut, S. C., Teague, G. B., and Beaudett, M. S. "Diagnosis of Alcohol Use Disorders in Schizophrenia." *Schizophrenia Bulletin,* 1990, *16,* 57–67.

Drake, R. E., Osher, F. C., and Wallach, M. A. "Alcohol Use and Abuse in Schizophrenia: A Prospective Community Study." *Journal of Nervous and Mental Disease,* 1989, *177,* 408–414.

Drake, R. E., and Wallach, M. A. "Moderate Drinking Among People with Severe Mental Illness." *Hospital and Community Psychiatry,* 1993, *44,* 780–782.

Drake, R. E., Yovetich, N. A., Bebout, R. R., Harris, M., and McHugo, G. J. "Integrated Treatment for Dually Diagnosed, Homeless Adults." Unpublished manuscript, 1996.

Galletely, C. A., Field, C. D., and Prior, M. "Urine Drug Screening of Patients Admitted to a State Psychiatric Hospital." *Hospital and Community Psychiatry,* 1993, *44,* 587–589.

Gold, M. S., and Dackis, C. A. "Role of the Laboratory in Evaluation of Suspected Drug Abusers." *Journal of Clinical Psychiatry,* 1986, *47,* 17–23.

Goldfinger, S. M., Schutt, R. K., Seidman, L. M., Turner, W. M., Penk, W. E., and Tolomiczenko, G. "Alternative Measures of Substance Abuse Among Homeless Mentally Ill Persons in Cross-Section and over Time." *Journal of Nervous and Mental Disease,* in press.

Goodman, L. A., Dutton, M. A., and Harris, M. "Physical and Sexual Assault Prevalence Among Homeless Women with Serious Mental Illness." *American Journal of Orthopsychiatry,* 1995, *65,* 468–478.

Grant, B. F. "Prevalence of the Proposed DSM-IV Alcohol Use Disorders: United States, 1988." *British Journal of Addiction,* 1992, *87,* 309–316.

Harris, M. "Treating Sexual Abuse Trauma with Dually Diagnosed Women." *Community Mental Health Journal,* in press.

Haywood, T. W., Kravitz, H. M., Grossman, L. S., Cavanaugh, J. L., Davis, J. M., and Lewis, D. A. "Predicting the 'Revolving Door' Phenomenon Among Patients with Schizophrenic, Schizoaffective, and Affective Disorders." *American Journal of Psychiatry,* 1995, *152,* 856–861.

Jerrell, J. M., and Ridgely, M. S. "Comparative Effectiveness of Three Approaches to Serving People with Severe Mental Illness and Substance Abuse Disorders." *Journal of Nervous and Mental Disease,* 1995, *183,* 566–576.

Knudsen, P., and Vilmar, T. "Cannabis and Neuroleptic Agents in Schizophrenia." *Acta Psychiatrica Scandinavica,* 1984, *69,* 162–174.

Kofoed, L. L. "Assessment of Comorbid Substance Abuse and Other Major Psychiatric Illnesses." In K. Minkoff and R. E. Drake (eds.), *Dual Diagnosis of Major Mental Illness and Substance Disorder.* New Directions for Mental Health Services, no. 50. San Francisco: Jossey-Bass, 1991, 43–55.

Lehman, A. F., and Dixon, L. (eds.) *Double Jeopardy: Chronic Mental Illness and Substance Abuse.* New York: Harwood Academic Publishers, 1995.

Lehman, A. F., Myers, P., and Corty, E. "Assessment and Classification of Patients with Psychiatric and Substance Abuse Syndromes." *Hospital and Community Psychiatry,* 1989, *40,* 1019–1025.

Lehman, A. F., Myers, C. P., Corty, E., and Thompson, J. "Severity of Substance-Use Disorders Among Psychiatric Inpatients." *Journal of Nervous and Mental Disease,* 1994, *182,* 164–167.

Lehman, A. F., Myers, C. P., Thompson, J. W., and Corty, E. "Implications of Mental and Substance Use Disorders: A Comparison of Single and Dual Diagnosis Patients." *Journal of Nervous and Mental Disease,* 1993, *181,* 365–370.

Lieberman, J. A., Kinon, B. J., and Loebel, A. D. "Dopaminergic Mechanisms in Idiopathic and Drug-Induced Psychoses." *Schizophrenia Bulletin,* 1990, *16,* 97–110.

McHugo, G. J., Drake, R. E., Burton, H. L., and Ackerson, T. M. "A Scale for Assessing the Stage of Substance Abuse Treatment in Persons with Severe Mental Illness." *Journal of Nervous and Mental Disease,* 1995, *183,* 762–767.

Magliozzi, J. R., Kanter, S. L., Csernansky, J. G., and Hollister, L. E. "Detection of Marijuana Use in Psychiatric Patients by Determination of Urinary Delta-9-Tetrahydrocannabino-11-oic acid." *Journal of Nervous and Mental Disease,* 1983, *171,* 246–249.

Marcus, P., and Snyder, R. "Reduction of Comorbid Substance Abuse with Clozapine." *American Journal of Psychiatry,* 1995, *142,* 959.

Minkoff, K., and Drake, R. E. (eds.). *Dual Diagnosis of Major Mental Illness and Substance Disorder.* New Directions for Mental Health Services, no. 50. San Francisco: Jossey-Bass, 1991.

Monti, P. M., Abrams, D. B., Kadden, R. M., and Cooney, N. L. *Treating Alcohol Dependence.* New York: Guilford Press, 1989.

Mueser, K. T., Nishith, P., Tracey, J. I., DeGirolamo, J., and Molinaro, M. "Expectations and Motives for Substance Use in Schizophrenia." *Schizophrenia Bulletin,* 1995, *21,* 367–378.

Mueser, K. T., Yarnold, P. R., and Bellack, A. S. "Diagnostic and Demographic Correlates of Substance Abuse in Schizophrenia and Major Affective Disorder." *Acta Psychiatrica Scandinavica,* 1992, *85,* 48–55.

Negrete, J. C., and Knapp, W. P. "The Effects of Cannabis Use on the Clinical Conditions of Schizophrenics." In L. S. Harris (ed.), *Problems of Drug Dependence.* Rockville, Md.: National Institute on Drug Abuse, 1986.

Noordsy, D. L., Drake, R. E., Biesanz, J. C., and McHugo, G. J. "Family History of Alcoholism in Schizophrenia." *Journal of Nervous and Mental Disease,* 1994, *182,* 651–655.

Noordsy, D. L., Schwab, B., Fox, L., and Drake, R. E. "The Role of Self-Help Programs in the Rehabilitation of Persons with Severe Mental Disorders and Substance Use Disorders." *Community Mental Health Journal,* 1996, *32,* 71–81.

Osher, F. C. and Kofoed, L. L. "Treatment of Patients with Both Psychiatric and Psychoactive Substance Use Disorders." *Hospital and Community Psychiatry,* 1989, *40,* 1025–1030.

Prochaska, J. O., DiClemente, C. C., and Norcross, J. C. "In Search of How People Change: Applications to Addictive Behaviors." *American Psychologist,* 1992, *47,* 1102–1114.

Regier, D. A., Farmer, M. E., Rae, D. S., Locke, B. Z., Keith, S. J., Judd, L. L., and Goodwin, F. K. "Comorbidity of Mental Disorders with Alcohol and Other Drug Abuse." *Journal of the American Medical Association,* 1990, *264,* 2511–2518.

Richard, M. L., Liskow, B. I., and Perry, P. J. "Recent Psychostimulant Use in Hospitalized Schizophrenics." *Journal of Clinical Psychiatry,* 1985, *46,* 79–83.

Ridgely, M. S., Osher, F. C., and Talbott, S. A. *Chronically Mentally Ill Young Adults with Substance Abuse Problems: Treatment and Training Issues.* Rockville, Md.: Alcohol, Drug Abuse, and Mental Health Administration, 1987.

Rosenberg, S. D., Drake, R. E., and Mueser, K. T., "New Directions for Treatment Research on Sequelae of Sexual Abuse in Persons with Severe Mental Illness." *Community Mental Health Journal,* in press.

Ryglewicz, H. "Psychoeducation for Clients and Families: A Way In, Out, and Through in Working with People with Dual Disorders." *Psychosocial Rehabilitation Journal,* 1991, *15,* 79–89.

Safer, D. J. "Substance Abuse by Young Adult Chronic Patients." *Hospital and Community Psychiatry,* 1987, *38,* 511–514.

Selzer, M. L. "The Michigan Alcoholism Screening Test: The Quest for a New Diagnostic Instrument." *American Journal of Psychiatry,* 1971, *127,* 89–94.

Shaner, A., Khaka, E., Roberts, L., Wilkins, J., Anglin, D., and Hsieh, S. "Unrecognizable Cocaine Use Among Schizophrenic Patients." *American Journal of Psychiatry,* 1993, *150,* 758–762.

Skinner, H. A. "The Drug Abuse Screening Test." *Addictive Behaviors,* 1982, *7,* 363–371.

Skinner, H., Holt, S., Sheu, W. J., and Israel, Y. "Clinical Versus Laboratory Detection of Alcohol Abuse: The Alcohol Clinical Index." *British Medical Journal*, 1986, *292*, 2261–2265.

Sobell, M. B., Maisto, S. A., Sobell, L. C., Cooper, A. M., Cooper, T., and Sanders, B. "Developing a Prototype for Evaluating Alcohol Treatment Effectiveness. In L. C. Sobell, M. B. Sobell, and E. Ward (eds.), *Evaluating Alcohol and Drug Abuse Effectiveness*. New York: Pergamon, 1980, 129–150.

Spitzer, R. L., Williams, J.B.W., Gibbon, M. and First, B. B. *Structured Clinical Interview for DSM-III-R-Patient Version (SCID-P)*. New York: Biometric Research Department, New York State Psychiatric Institute, 1988.

Stone, A., Greenstein, R., Gamble, G., and McLellan, A. T. "Cocaine Use in Chronic Schizophrenic Outpatients Receiving Depot Neuroleptic Medications." *Hospital and Community Psychiatry*, 1993, *44*, 176–177.

Test, M. A., Wallisch, L. S., Allness, D. J., and Ripp, K. "Substance Use in Young Adults with Schizophrenic Disorders." *Schizophrenia Bulletin*, 1989, *15*, 465–476.

Toland, A. M., and Moss, H. B. "Identification of the Alcoholic Schizophrenic: Use of Clinical Laboratory Tests and the MAST." *Journal of Studies on Alcohol*, 1989, *50*, 49–53.

Yesavage, J. A., and Zarcone, V. "History of Drug Abuse and Dangerous Behavior in Inpatient Schizophrenics." *Journal of Clinical Psychiatry*, 1983, *44*, 259–261.

*ROBERT E. DRAKE, M.D., Ph.D., is professor of psychiatry and community and family medicine at Dartmouth Medical School and director of the New Hampshire–Dartmouth Psychiatric Research Center.*

*STANLEY D. ROSENBERG, Ph.D., is professor of psychiatry and director of the psychology internship training program at Dartmouth Medical School.*

*KIM T. MUESER, Ph.D., is associate professor of psychiatry and community and family medicine at Dartmouth Medical School and a senior researcher at the New Hampshire–Dartmouth Psychiatric Research Center.*

*A model for the treatment of co-occurring substance abuse and major
mental disorders is proposed. The model integrates empirically
grounded strategies applicable to substance abuse problems into
the context of outpatient mental health treatment.*

# Treatment of Co-Occurring Substance Abuse and Major Mental Illness

*Kate B. Carey*

Mark is a twenty-three-year-old single white male diagnosed with schizophrenia and both cocaine and marijuana dependence. Mark has already experienced multiple psychiatric admissions necessitated by acute psychotic symptoms and violent behavior. Urinalysis results indicated that cocaine use probably precipitated these episodes. Mark repeatedly refused referrals to inpatient drug rehabilitation programs and would not attend local Double Trouble meetings. He boasted of his drug use and stated that he had no reason to stop using because he had already damaged his brain.

He began a course of outpatient treatment with a therapist experienced with major mental disorders who also was a certified substance abuse counselor. Mark attended therapy irregularly for over a year and continued to use marijuana almost daily and cocaine episodically. Attendance gradually became more regular and Mark became more self-revealing as his trust in his therapist grew. He admitted feeling painfully different from other people, ashamed of his disorder, and felt socially awkward and isolated. Mark and the therapist identified a recurring pattern: when his despair and anger mounted, he would discontinue medication and increase his drug use. This usually resulted in family discord and hospitalization. His therapist engaged Mark in nonjudgmental discussions about his perceived advantages of continuing to use drugs (these included feeling normal, temporary relief from anger, social contacts with other drug users), as well as the disadvantages of continuing to use (for instance, not having money to spend on material goods, inpatient admissions reminding him of being different). Abstinence from drug use seemed frightening and

Preparation of this chapter was supported by National Institute of Drug Abuse Grant
DA07635.

unattainable. Mark's therapist expressed faith in him and encouraged him to take it one day at a time; at one point, he called her to announce the completion of a full day of sobriety.

Over time, Mark spoke of disappointments in attaining the things that so many of his peers enjoyed, such as a job, marriage, and having a car. His therapist helped him articulate his own short-term goals (for instance, getting a stereo and his own apartment) and the necessary steps to attain them. At present, Mark has obtained housing in a group home for mentally ill substance abusers and is working toward more independent living. His treatment plan spells out progressively increasing privileges, including more responsibility for managing his money, contingent upon his attendance at self-help groups and following house rules. He continues to use marijuana periodically, but has not used cocaine in six months. Mark is developing skills that help him identify mood states and social situations that place him at high risk for using drugs. Both he and his therapist monitor these situations and rehearse alternative action plans designed to help him avoid drug use.

## A Model for Treating Dually Diagnosed Clients

Persons with major (Axis I) mental disorders have three times the risk of alcohol or drug abuse problems than those without mental disorders (Regier and others, 1990). Among certain diagnostic groups such as schizophrenia, prevalence of substance use disorders approaches 50 percent (Mueser and others, 1990; Test, Wallisch, Allness, and Ripp, 1989). Thus persons with major mental disorders represent an extremely high risk group for substance abuse problems.

Because the vast majority of persons with Axis I disorders receive treatment in the mental health system, treatment providers must be prepared to incorporate substance abuse assessment and treatment planning into the overall care of their clients. Furthermore, the bulk of treatment for these co-occurring disorders takes place on an outpatient basis. This means that treatment is implemented in environments where substances may be readily available and various triggers for substance use continue to be present. Treatment providers need guidelines for addressing substance abuse behaviors that are consistent with the mental health treatment process and that offer the option for client-therapist collaboration on mutually acceptable goals.

I have proposed a heuristic, five-step model for structuring treatment of dual-diagnosis clients (Carey, in press). Several assumptions underlie this treatment approach. First, the model assumes an outpatient mental-health context in which clients have contact with a primary therapist or case manager. Second, the model attempts to integrate substance abuse interventions and ongoing psychiatric treatment. This approach contrasts to alternative approaches that provide substance abuse treatment either sequentially or in parallel (often in different settings) with psychiatric treatment. Third, I acknowledge that comprehensive treatment for co-occurring disorders usually requires a combination of pharmacological treatment, psychosocial treatments (both individual and group interventions), and supportive services (for example, case management, housing, family education). This model focuses primarily on psychosocial interventions (see Mueser and Noordsy, this volume). The fourth and final assumption of the proposed model consists of adopting a longitudinal approach to treatment. Both types of disorders tend to be chronic and relapsing problems. A single trial of intensive treatment is unlikely to achieve lasting change. Thus treatment goals may consist of abstinence from nonprescribed drugs and alcohol and stability or remission of psychiatric symptoms. Success, however, will usually be measured in terms of approximation to those goals achieved in the context of a long-term treatment relationship.

This model is organized around five therapeutic tasks or steps that can serve as guidelines for treatment planning. The five steps are: establishing a working alliance, evaluating the cost-benefit ratio of continued substance use, individualizing goals for changes in substance use, building an environment and lifestyle supportive of abstinence, and anticipating and coping with crises. Although these steps are ordered in a typically occurring sequence, they do not need to be implemented in rigid order. Rather they provide a schema for integrating treatment planning for substance use reduction into ongoing treatment for major mental disorders. The uniqueness of each client with regard to problem areas, behavioral skills, and readiness to change will determine how much time may be spent in each area. Each step will be described in detail and relevant strategies for accomplishing each task will be offered.

## Establishing a Working Alliance

Building a therapeutic alliance may take months or even years. Establishing a relationship between the client and a member of the treatment team, however, constitutes a critical first step toward changing substance use patterns. During this relationship-building period, the treatment provider must communicate a sincere acceptance of the person, although not necessarily his or her substance use behavior. A major goal is to establish trust, which is a prerequisite for the client to openly talk about substance use and the role that alcohol and drugs play in the client's life. Trust-building time serves two purposes. The therapist gains credibility and reinforcement value (if the client believes that the therapist is sincerely committed to his/her welfare), and a safe environment is created for the client to express concerns and fears about changing. Such an environment helps to support the client through initial— perhaps physically and mentally painful—efforts to control substance use. Specific strategies to establish a working alliance include providing medications, assisting in obtaining entitlements, and helping with food and recreational opportunities.

Both clinical observations (Levy and Mann, 1988) and empirical evidence (Mueser, Drake, and Miles, in press; McHugo, Drake, Burton, and Ackerson, 1995) suggest that not all clients with co-occurring disorders are ready to accept substance use as a problem or to engage in active steps to reduce substance use. Relevant to understanding individual differences in readiness to change are the stages of change central to the Transtheoretical Model of Change (Prochaska and DiClemente, 1992). The primary stages of change applicable to addictive and other problem behaviors consist of precontemplation, contemplation, preparation, active change, and maintenance. Precontemplators do not admit to experiencing substance-related problems, contemplators are receptive to acknowledging problems but are ambivalent about change, persons in the preparation stage begin to make behavioral steps toward substance use reduction, persons engaged in active change have achieved some initial success, and persons in the maintenance stage continue to work on maintaining treatment gains. Different intervention strategies may be appropriate at each stage; for example, drink refusal skills training may be effective for individuals ready for active change or maintaining treatment gains; it may not be well-accepted, however, by persons in the precontemplation stage who have not yet decided that they need to refuse drinks. In general, behavioral strategies (for example, stimulus control, contingency management, or social support) are more effective in active change and maintenance stages, and cognitive or attitudinal interventions (for example, education, emotional expression, evaluating oneself in relationship to environment) are most effective for persons in precontemplation and contemplation stages (Prochaska, DiClemente, and Norcross, 1992).

The stages of change concepts just described are consistent with the Osher and Kofoed (1989) four-stage model of dual-diagnosis treatment (engagement, persuasion, active treatment, and relapse prevention). Based on the Osher and Kofoed stages, a Substance Abuse Treatment Scale (SATS) (McHugo, Drake, Burton, and Ackerson, 1995) has been developed to help clinicians and researchers rate the degree to which dually diagnosed clients recognize the need for and actively participate in substance abuse treatment. The SATS has been shown to be reliable and valid in this population and is sensitive to changes over time associated with involvement in treatment (McHugo, Drake, Burton, and Ackerson, 1995). Thus an assessment tool exists to monitor the extent to which a therapeutic alliance has been formed and, more broadly, the client's readiness to change substance abuse patterns.

Integrating the stages of change concepts into treatment for co-occurring substance use and psychiatric disorders can be very fruitful. For the large number of precontemplators and contemplators, spending time building a working alliance sets the stage for more aggressive treatment efforts. Thus the function of this step is to engage the client in treatment and maintain sufficient contact for additional therapeutic work (Osher and Kofoed, 1989). Clients in precontemplative stages of change may require more time in alliance building than clients in contemplative or active stages. Once the client has established a connection to, and faith in, someone on the treatment staff, then it is possible to exploit naturally occurring events, or windows of opportunity, that enhance the person's readiness to change.

## Evaluating Costs and Benefits
## of Continued Substance Use

The next step involves therapeutic activities designed to increase motivation for reducing substance use. These activities begin when the client is willing to discuss his or her substance use and the effects it has on his or her life. Clients are likely to be in the contemplation stage and therapeutic goals include persuading the client that substance use patterns have to change. To do this, useful strategies include education about substances and their effects, functional analysis assessment, articulation of life goals, and cost-benefit analysis.

The first activity relevant to this step is providing accurate information about the short- and long-term effects of substance use, and specifically about their effects on cognitive, emotional, and behavioral symptoms experienced by the client. Although this type of education may be initiated by the therapist, the effectiveness of the message may be enhanced if the information is provided when relevant to issues raised by the client. For example, if complaints of increased anxiety appear to be temporally related to evidence of cocaine use, the therapist may encourage speculation about the causal relations and offer a brief discussion of cocaine-induced physical and psychological changes.

Educational interventions alone rarely result in behavior change. Knowledge can serve to set the stage by raising awareness of consequences attributable to substance use rather than other causes, however (psychiatric or medical problems, for example). Furthermore, this process can help to identify and challenge inaccurate beliefs about substances.

The second activity that can be useful at this step is to conduct a functional analysis of substance use. A functional analysis is an assessment strategy that attempts to make explicit the functional relationships between the antecedents of substance use (thoughts, feelings, situations), the use of alcohol and drugs, and the consequences of substance use (Haynes and O'Brien, 1990; Sobell, Sobell, and Nirenberg, 1988). Substance use patterns would thus first be carefully assessed, then attention would be devoted to the types of cognitive, emotional, interpersonal, and environmental events that are associated with increased and decreased substance use. Many events thought to precipitate substance use in persons with major mental disorders, such as cognitive distortions, emotional turmoil, or social isolation and discomfort, can easily be conceptualized as antecedents for substance use. Careful assessment of both the short- and long-term consequences can reveal sources of reinforcement that maintain substance use. Stasiewicz, Carey, Bradizza, and Maisto (in press) provide an illustrative case example of functional analysis of alcohol and drug use in a client with major depressive disorder.

The utility of a functional analysis is twofold. When conducted in a context of information gathering, it can educate both client and therapist about the role that substances play in the client's life. Often substance use serves significant functions, including social facilitation, relief from unpleasant emotions, changes in cognitive states (for instance, ruminations, racing thoughts, uncomfortable self-focus), and promoting a certain self-image or feelings of control (Dixon, Haas, Weiden, Sweeney, and Frances, 1990). As therapists, we must respect the functions of substance use and validate the needs underlying the desire to use. The needs can be distinguished, though, from the methods used to achieve them. The functional analysis can also reveal differences between perceived and real benefits and short- and long-term consequences. This discrepancy can serve to illustrate the ultimate ineffectiveness of substances in achieving the very outcomes that motivate their use.

A third activity consists of identifying and discussing the client's life goals, such as getting an apartment or job or staying out of the hospital. It may take time for the client to articulate personal goals. Furthermore, the therapist may need to shape initially unrealistic goals into more appropriate forms. Goal setting is central to many models of motivation, and the greatest motivational impact occurs when goals are specific (rather than vague), proximal (rather than distal), and attainable (Miller, 1985). Goal setting also provides a focus for discussions about what must change in order for goals to be met. For psychiatric outpatients, substance use almost always interferes with attaining desired outcomes. Sometimes focusing on the goal (that requires a reduction in substance use) rather than focusing on the substance use is an effective strategy early in the change process.

These preliminary activities serve consciousness raising functions (see Prochaska, Velicer, DiClemente, and Fava, 1988, for further discussion of matching therapeutic processes to stages of change). The costs and benefits of continued substance use can now be addressed. Optimally, these should be elicited from the client because taking too active a role in identifying problems can create psychological reactance. *Reactance* refers to the oppositional way a person behaves when that person feels he or she is being influenced in a certain direction (Brehm and Brehm, 1981). Thus a person may resist acknowledging the costs of continued use if the therapist attempts to point them out. Miller and Rollnick (1991) offer a wealth of motivational interviewing strategies, such as open-ended questions, reflective listening, and elaboration, that can help to elicit such information. Over time, the therapist can reframe problems whenever possible (loss of housing, for example) to include the contributions of substance use, gradually increasing the lists of costs. Increased acknowledgment of the costs related to drinking distinguishes individuals ready for active change from those in earlier stages (King and DiClemente, 1993). The therapist can then relate the benefits and costs of substance use articulated by the client back to life goals. Maintaining a focus on desired goals is a way of integrating substance use with the many other therapeutic concerns addressed in outpatient mental health treatment.

In summary, the tasks discussed in this section serve as groundwork for substance abuse treatment planning. Within an ongoing treatment relationship, clients can learn accurate information about substance effects, begin talking about substance use patterns and their relationships to other aspects of their lives, verbalize realistic goals, relate changes in substance use to achieving desired outcomes, and ultimately identify both the benefits and costs of substance use. These tasks also help to move clients toward greater readiness to change.

## Individualizing Goals for Change

Although outcome goals for persons with psychiatric disorders have not been studied empirically, it is generally assumed that abstinence from nonprescribed drugs and alcohol is the optimal outcome for psychiatrically impaired substance abusers. However, many substance abusers are unwilling or unable to make a complete commitment to lifelong abstinence. The harm-reduction approach provides an alternative to traditional abstinence-oriented philosophies, and is more likely to engage persons who will not or cannot embrace abstinence as a goal (Marlatt and Tapert, 1993). Underlying harm reduction is the notion that substance use exists on a continuum of abstinence to abuse. If a person successfully reduces the quantity and frequency of substance use, the likelihood of suffering negative consequences should also decrease—any movement in the direction of reduced use should be encouraged. Importantly, adopting a harm-reduction attitude in treatment does not reject abstinence outcomes; rather, it accepts other outcomes (often on the way to abstinence) if they represent a reduction in the risks associated with substance use. Abstinence may continue to be the desired goal, but flexibility in short-term goals represents a collaborative approach that may enhance the involvement of abusers in treatment.

For persons who use drugs or alcohol irregularly, initial goals may be to use less often or to use smaller amounts. For persons who have been unable to voluntarily abstain in the past, twenty-four hours of abstinence may constitute a reasonable initial goal. Noticeable changes in pattern, such as interrupting "using days" with brief strings of sober days may represent significant progress consistent with the harm-reduction objective. The effort should be recognized so that the client may feel an enhanced sense of self-efficacy and control over substance use. Feelings of personal efficacy are central to many psychological models of change (Bandura, 1986; Marlatt and Gordon, 1985).

It has been proposed that a therapist's willingness to individualize treatment goals may encourage more clients to modify their substance use patterns than a strict abstinence-only, "zero tolerance" approach. Establishing meaningful but attainable goals for substance use reduction or abstinence can be considered the first step in the evolution of control over the role substances play in a person's life. First steps, however, can be intimidating and sometimes painful. A collaborative alliance between client and treatment staff can help to ensure that initial efforts are reinforced and perceived as success experiences.

## Building an Environment and Lifestyle
## Supportive of Abstinence

In light of the pervasive dysfunction associated with co-occurring disorders, exclusive focus on the abusing individual will result in limited success. Personal efforts to change substance use behaviors must be paralleled by social and environmental changes that reinforce abstinence. Consequently the construction of these supports is an essential part of treatment planning.

The treatment program constitutes one such source of support and reinforcement for abstinence. During early stages of change, as much structure as possible should be provided to the client in the form of a day treatment program or frequent clinic appointments. This structure serves several purposes: it encourages regular contact with others who support recovery efforts, it maximizes the time spent in drug-free environments, and it helps to fill the void left when clients avoid drug-related activities. However, treatment contact is inherently limited, and should be supplemented by additional social supports.

Typically, sources of environmental support for recovery include family, work, church, and community groups. Many chronically mentally ill persons are not well-integrated into these naturally occurring support systems, however. Consequently they may feel that they have little to lose by continuing their substance abuse. In fact, they may not be reinforced for sobriety unless environmental and lifestyle restructuring is part of the treatment plan. When available, family members can be apprised of the treatment plan and encouraged to provide moral support as well as tangible assistance (transportation and meals, for instance) contingent upon sobriety (see Clark, this volume). Clients can be encouraged to rebuild connections to other support systems where such connections had previously existed (for example, rejoin a congregation or use vocational skills on a part-time or volunteer basis). In cases where nondrug support systems had never been in place, a more fundamental skills building approach must be taken. Basic interpersonal, time management, leisure, and work-related skills must be incorporated into the treatment plan to enable clients to pursue abstinence-promoting environments and relationships.

Building social support for abstinence may require avoidance of peers if these individuals also abuse substances. Ample evidence suggests that one of the strongest predictors of substance use is a substance-abusing peer group (Murray and Perry, 1985). Thus, recovery may be undermined if clients continue to associate with persons who abuse alcohol or drugs. Replacing friends and related social activities is difficult, especially for persons with poor social skills. Many recovering persons experience loneliness (Akerlind and Hornquist, 1992), which suggests that establishing social supports and rebuilding social networks during recovery is a particularly important challenge.

Recovering persons often need help in finding activities to structure time that had previously been occupied with substance-related behaviors. This task often requires a great deal of creativity given both the limited number of opportunities offered by communities for meaningful involvement by mentally ill members and the unpredictability of the recovery process. Ideas for activities that the client finds enjoyable may emerge during alliance-building stages and may include recreational activities, volunteer work, and educational or training opportunities.

Self-help groups can provide both social support and structured activities. Not all persons with psychiatric disorders find self-help groups tolerable or helpful, however (Noordsy, Schwab, Fox, and Drake, 1996). Clients with schizophrenia are less likely to attend than those with other diagnoses, suggesting that social skills deficits may limit the benefits received from self-help group attendance. Nonetheless, most dually diagnosed clients should be encouraged to try at least a couple of meetings. Treatment staff may want to accompany clients to their first meetings in order to help them overcome initial intimidation. Clients whose symptoms or behaviors get in the way of participation in community groups may want to seek out Double Trouble groups, which are created for persons with both mental illness and addiction problems. In addition, some treatment sites have experimented with Alcoholics Anonymous–preparation groups (see Mueser and Noordsy, this volume) to acquaint clients with some of the rituals of self-help meetings and to anticipate potential difficulties they may experience. Note that models have been developed for modified step work tailored to various psychiatric disorders that can supplement (or in some cases substitute for) twelve-step oriented self-help groups (for example, Evans and Sullivan, 1990).

Finally, an environment supportive of abstinence must also include the client's residence. Every attempt should be made to create a drug-free living environment. Supportive housing that does not tolerate substance use can provide needed external limits on one's own as well as others' behavior. In essence, housing often gives a client "something to lose" if substance use gets out of control.

In summary, recovery attempts involve a transaction between personal commitment and effort and an environment that supports and promotes a healthier lifestyle. Neither component alone is sufficient for lasting change to take place. Persons with psychiatric disorders may need additional assistance to manage necessary lifestyle changes if they experience deficits in interpersonal relationships or in organization and planning skills.

## Coping with Crises

Substance use disorders and most major mental illnesses are relapsing disorders. Both treatment traditions incorporate relapse prevention concepts (see Marlatt and Gordon, 1985); in the case of coexisting disorders, relapse prevention is broadly defined to address setbacks in both. Commonly, relapse in one domain can trigger relapse in the other. Acknowledging that recovery is usually a long-term process interrupted by periodic relapses, several authors advocate a continuum-of-care plan for dual-diagnosis clients (for example, Carey, 1989;

Drake, Teague, and Warren, 1990). Access to detoxification, psychiatric evaluation for medication adjustments, inpatient psychiatric hospitalization, or temporary housing may be periodically necessary, and coordinated management of such transitions helps to limit the scope of inevitable setbacks. Thus treatment planning should anticipate relapses and should prepare to cope with crises.

The causes of relapse among recovering substance abusers with psychiatric disorders include biological, psychological, and social factors (Evans and Sullivan, 1990). Biological factors include withdrawal symptoms that trigger substance use to counteract discomfort, a poor response to psychiatric medications that leaves a client symptomatic, an extroverted temperament prone to sensation seeking, and extreme physiological states (such as being hungry, angry, lonely, tired, or sick). Psychological factors include negative emotional states, positive expectations of drug effects, patterns of distorted thinking (for example, "I can't do anything right"), and an impoverished lifestyle that provides little meaningful engagement with anything other than substance use and its rituals. Social factors include peer pressure to drink or use drugs, holidays or social occasions associated with substance use, and interpersonal conflict. These are notably consistent with relapse typologies developed from studies of primary substance abusers (Marlatt and Gordon, 1985).

The functional analysis conducted earlier in the treatment process should yield information about situations in which substances have been used in the past, and the needs that alcohol and other drugs have typically met. Thus it is often possible to anticipate the types of situations that are likely to precipitate relapse for individual clients. Relapse prevention, broadly defined, is a collaborative process in which the client tries to identify and cope with difficult events, and the treatment staff offers early intervention to reduce the harm if a relapse does occur. With regard to substance use, staff can reinforce continued contact with treatment after periods of use and help to evaluate what happened and why. Thus relapses should not be seen as failures but as opportunities to learn. Similarly, early signs of psychiatric decompensation can be monitored, medications can be reevaluated, and sources of stress can be identified before the desire to resort to chemical management becomes overwhelming.

A key component of relapse prevention consists of coping-skills training. Because substance use has often served important coping functions, clients must learn to cope with substance-related triggers in new ways. According to Nikkel (1994), persons with co-occurring disorders can benefit from enhancement of a variety of skills, including communication and social skills, mood and stress management skills, medication and symptom management skills, and other daily living skills. Skills training models are well-suited to this population because these interventions provide a clear definition of skills to be learned, modeling of target skills by group leaders, behavioral rehearsal, and corrective feedback on the implementation of skills. Not surprisingly, enhancement of adaptive function through skills training interventions enjoys extensive empirical support among both psychiatric (Liberman, DeRisi, and Mueser, 1989) and substance abuse clients (Monti, Abrams, Kadden, and Cooney, 1989).

Coping with crises refers to the active, ongoing process of anticipating the multiple determinants of relapse and coping with setbacks as they occur, optimally within a continuum of comprehensive care. Work with mentally ill substance abusers requires a broad definition of relapse that encompasses both psychiatric and substance abuse setbacks, because outcomes of each are mutually dependent. If relapses are framed within a collaborative learning experience, they can serve to refocus treatment efforts toward high-risk areas. Coping-skills training can be employed when skills deficits contribute to relapse risk. Importantly, both clients and treatment staff should expect to participate in a longitudinal recovery process.

## Conclusion

The substance-abuse treatment model just described can be individualized for clients with varying degrees and types of psychopathology, as well as those with different degrees of willingness and ability to change. This model explicitly addresses the early stages of change in which clients must be engaged in a helping relationship and persuaded that substance abuse should be a focus of treatment. These stages receive relatively little attention in the treatment literature, as most substance-abuse treatment models emphasize activities relevant to active change and relapse prevention stages.

The proposed model incorporates several additional components that distinguish it from standard approaches to substance abuse treatment. First, it recognizes that the process of recovery from co-occurring disorders requires a *longitudinal perspective*. This contrasts with the finite duration of many substance-abuse treatment programs. For persons with limited social and psychological resources, and with destabilizing relapses caused by psychiatric disorders interfering with a recovery focus, a long-term treatment model appears essential. Second, this model advocates an *integrated treatment approach*, fully incorporating substance use behaviors and consequences into the bigger picture of psychiatric treatment. Because these disorders are interdependent with regard to both symptom expression and the process of recovery, efforts to compartmentalize treatment may have limited success. Finally, the proposed model allows for flexibility in defining successful outcomes. The *harm reduction philosophy* (contrasted with the zero-tolerance philosophy) provides more opportunities for success experiences and tries to avoid unrealistic goals that set clients up for failure. Furthermore, encouraging therapists to perceive incremental change may enhance their sense of accomplishment when working with very challenging clients.

In sum, a five-step model for reducing substance use within the context of outpatient psychiatric treatment has been proposed. The influence of themes from the psychological treatment literature appears throughout the model; these include stages of change, harm reduction, and motivational interventions. Such cross-fertilization promises to improve services available to the challenging population of dually diagnosed clients.

# References

Akerlind, I., and Hornquist, J. O. "Loneliness and Alcohol Abuse: A Review of Evidence of an Interplay." *Social Science and Medicine,* 1992, *34,* 405–414.

Bandura, A. *Social Foundations of Thought and Action: A Social Cognitive Theory.* Englewood Cliffs, N.J.: Prentice-Hall, 1986.

Brehm, S. S., and Brehm, J. W. *Psychological Reactance: A Theory of Freedom and Control.* New York: Academic Press, 1981.

Carey, K. B. "Treatment of the Mentally Ill Chemical Abuser: Description of the Hutchings Day Treatment Program." *Psychiatric Quarterly,* 1989, *60,* 303–316.

Carey, K. B. "Substance Use Reduction in the Context of Outpatient Psychiatric Treatment: A Collaborative, Motivational, Harm Reduction Approach." *Community Mental Health Journal,* in press.

Dixon, L., Haas, G., Weiden, P., Sweeney, J., and Frances, A. "Acute Effects of Drug Abuse in Schizophrenic Patients: Clinical Observations and Patients' Self-Reports." *Schizophrenia Bulletin,* 1990, *16,* 69–79.

Drake, R. E., Teague, G. B., and Warren, S. R. "Dual Diagnosis: The New Hampshire Program." *Addiction and Recovery,* 1990, June, 35–39.

Evans, K., and Sullivan, J. M. *Dual Diagnosis: Counseling the Mentally Ill Substance Abuser.* New York: Guilford Press, 1990.

Haynes, S. N., and O'Brien, W. H. "Functional Analysis in Behavior Therapy." *Clinical Psychology Review,* 1990, *10,* 649–668.

King, T. K., and DiClemente, C. C. "A Decisional Balance Measure for Assessing and Predicting Drinking Behavior." Poster presented at the annual meeting of the Association for Advancement of Behavior Therapy, Atlanta, November 1993.

Levy, M. S., and Mann, D. W. "The Special Treatment Team: An Inpatient Approach to the Mentally Ill Alcoholic Patient." *Journal of Substance Abuse Treatment,* 1988, *5,* 219–227.

Liberman, R. P., DeRisi, W. J., and Mueser, K. T. *Social Skills Training for Psychiatric Patients.* Elmsford, N.Y.: Pergamon, 1989.

Marlatt, G. A., and Gordon, J. R. *Relapse Prevention: Maintenance Strategies in the Treatment of Addictive Behaviors.* New York: Guilford Press, 1985.

Marlatt, G. A., and Tapert, S. F. "Harm Reduction: Reducing the Risks of Addictive Behaviors." In J. S. Baer, G. A. Marlatt, and R. J. McMahon (eds.), *Addictive Behaviors Across the Lifespan: Prevention, Treatment, and Policy Issues.* Newbury Park, Calif.: Sage, 1993.

McHugo, G. J., Drake, R. E., Burton, H. L., and Ackerson, T. H. "A Scale for Assessing the Stage of Substance Abuse Treatment in Persons with Severe Mental Illness." *Journal of Nervous and Mental Disease,* 1995, *183,* 762–767.

Miller, W. R. "Motivation for Treatment: A Review with Special Emphasis on Alcoholism." *Psychological Bulletin,* 1985, *98,* 84–107.

Miller, W. R., and Rollnick, S. *Motivational Interviewing: Preparing People to Change Addictive Behavior.* New York: Guilford Press, 1991.

Monti, P. M., Abrams, D. B., Kadden, R. M., and Cooney, N. L. *Treating Alcohol Dependence.* New York: Guilford Press, 1989.

Mueser, K. T., Drake, R. E., and Miles, K. M. "The Course and Treatment of Substance Use Disorder in Persons with Severe Mental Illness." In *NIDA Research Monograph: Comorbid Mental and Addictive Disorders: Treatment and HIV-Related Issues.* Rockville, Md.: U.S. Department of Health and Human Services, in press.

Mueser, K. T., Yarnold, P. R., Levinson, D. F., Singh, H., Bellack, A. S., Kee, K., Morrison, R. L., and Yadalam, K. G. "Prevalence of Substance Abuse in Schizophrenia: Demographic and Clinical Correlates." *Schizophrenia Bulletin,* 1990, *16,* 31–56.

Murray, D. M., and Perry, C. L. "The Prevention of Adolescent Drug Abuse: Implications of Etiological, Developmental, Behavioral, and Environmental Models." In C. L. Jones and R. J. Battjes (eds.), *Etiology of Drug Abuse: Implications for Treatment* (Department of Health and Human Services no. ADM 85-1335). Washington, D.C.: U.S. Government Printing Office, 1985.

Nikkel, R. E. "Areas of Skill Training for Persons with Mental Illness and Substance Use Disorders: Building Skills for Successful Community Living." *Community Mental Health Journal*, 1994, *30*, 61–72.

Noordsy, D. L., Schwab, B., Fox, L., and Drake, R. E. "The Role of Self-Help Programs in the Rehabilitation of Persons with Severe Mental Illness and Substance Use Disorder." *Community Mental Health Journal*, 1996, *32*, 71–81.

Osher, F. C., and Kofoed, L. L. "Treatment of Patients with Psychiatric and Psychoactive Substance Abuse Disorders." *Hospital and Community Psychiatry*, 1989, *40*, 1025–1030.

Prochaska, J. O., and DiClemente, C. C. "Stages of Change in the Modification of Problem Behaviors." In M. Hersen, R. M. Eisler, and P. M. Miller (eds.), *Progress in Behavior Modification*. Newbury Park, Calif.: Sage, 1992.

Prochaska, J. O., DiClemente, C. C., and Norcross, J. C. "In Search of How People Change: Applications to Addictive Behaviors." *American Psychologist*, 1992, *47*, 1102–1114.

Prochaska, J. O., Velicer, W. F., DiClemente, C. C., and Fava, J. "Measuring Processes of Change: Application to the Cessation of Smoking." *Journal of Consulting and Clinical Psychology*, 1988, *56*, 520–528.

Regier, D. A., Farmer, M. E., Rae, D. S., Locke, B. Z., Keith, S. J., Judd, L. L., and Goodwin, F. K. "Comorbidity of Mental Disorders with Alcohol and Other Drug Abuse." *Journal of the American Medical Association*, 1990, *264*, 2511–2518.

Sobell, L. C., Sobell, M. B., and Nirenberg, T. D. "Behavioral Assessment and Treatment Planning with Alcohol and Drug Abusers: A Review with an Emphasis on Clinical Applications." *Clinical Psychology Review*, 1988, *8*, 19–54.

Stasiewicz, P., Carey, K., Bradizza, C., and Maisto, S. "Behavioral Assessment of Substance Abuse with Co-Occurring Psychiatric Disorder." *Cognitive and Behavioral Practice*, in press.

Test, M. A., Wallisch, L. S., Allness, D. J., and Ripp, K. "Substance Use in Young Adults with Schizophrenic Disorders." *Schizophrenia Bulletin*, 1989, *15*, 465–476.

KATE B. CAREY, Ph.D., is a licensed clinical psychologist and associate professor of psychology at Syracuse University in Syracuse, New York.

*Group treatment is a widely practiced intervention for persons with dual diagnoses. This chapter reviews the rationale for group treatment and discusses four different approaches to group intervention: twelve-step, educational-supportive, social skills, and stagewise treatment.*

# Group Treatment for Dually Diagnosed Clients

*Kim T. Mueser, Douglas L. Noordsy*

It is now widely accepted that dually diagnosed individuals require interventions that simultaneously address both mental health and substance use disorders. In addition to recognizing the need to treat both dual disorders when present, integrated treatment models have embraced the concept of *stages of recovery* from substance use disorder. Accordingly, treatment must motivate clients to address their substance abuse prior to attempting to reduce substance use (Miller and Rollnick, 1991; Prochaska, Velicer, DiClemente, and Fava, 1988). Drake and others (1993) have proposed four stages of treatment designed to provide maximally relevant interventions: engagement (client is not engaged in treatment), persuasion (client is engaged in treatment but is not convinced of the importance of reducing substance use), active treatment (client is attempting to reduce substance use), and relapse prevention (client has reduced or stopped substance use and is trying to prevent relapses). The stage concept provides a heuristic to clinicians by identifying the critical goals at each stage, and leads to the selection of stage-specific interventions (for example, at the persuasion stage the clinician works to establish awareness of the consequences of substance use).

A core component of integrated treatment programs is the inclusion of group-based intervention. There are three reasons for including group treatment. First, there is a strong tradition of nonprofessional self-help groups such as Alcoholics Anonymous (AA) in the primary addiction field. The group format is an ideal setting for capitalizing on the common need for support and identification shared by persons with an addiction. Second, substance abuse among psychiatric clients frequently occurs in a social context (Dixon and others, 1991; Test, Wallisch, Allness, and Ripp, 1989). Addressing substance use-related issues in a group setting makes it clear to clients that they are not alone and provides an opportunity for the sharing of experiences and coping strategies. Third, there are economical advantages to offering group therapy rather than individual therapy because less clinician time is required.

## Models of Group Treatment

Different approaches to group treatment can be divided into four general models: twelve-step, broad-based educational-supportive, social skills training, and stagewise. Although this categorization facilitates the discussion of different group methods, many interventions are hybrids of more than one model (for example, stagewise treatment may include elements of twelve-step, social skills training, and educational-supportive models). Furthermore, for group intervention to be effective it must be provided in the context of a comprehensive treatment program, including elements such as ongoing assessment, case management, and pharmacotherapy (Drake and others, 1993).

**Twelve-Step Models.** Twelve-step models are based on the self-help group approach popularized by AA and adapted for other substances or disorders (narcotics addiction or gambling, for instance). A number of different approaches to dual diagnosis include aspects of twelve-step programs, such as clinician-led groups that prepare clients for community AA-type meetings and consumer-led self-help meetings with a focus on individuals with dual diagnoses. The clinician-led models, described by Minkoff (1989) and Bartels and Thomas (1991), include twelve-step principles and philosophy adapted from the AA model blended with education and support for mental-illness management. Treatment is usually delivered by clinicians with some personal or professional experience with the twelve-step model working in a mental health system. Their focus is on integrating substance abuse treatment with mental health care. These groups promote supplementary attendance at AA meetings but attempt to deliver comprehensive treatment through the group to those who never attend.

**Professionally Assisted Pre-AA Group.** We have previously described the difficulty persons with dual disorders have linking to self-help groups for substance abuse (Noordsy, Schwab, Fox, and Drake, 1996). We therefore designed a pre-AA model of group treatment for the New Hampshire study of dual diagnosis. This model is designed to facilitate the linkage of clients to self-help treatment in the community by developing an awareness of the consequences of substance use, motivation for treatment, and familiarity with the twelve-step approach. Although initial work in this model parallels the persuasion model by necessity (see section on stagewise treatment on p. 37), the language and milieu of the group differ. Twelve-step concepts such as denial, rationalization, working the steps, and surrender are central to the pre-AA group but not in persuasion groups. Members are also encouraged to attend self-help meetings and listen to others' stories to further their motivation to change.

The group discusses typical barriers clients experience to attending self-help groups, such as social discomfort, the emphasis on religion, and the negative stance some AA members have toward psychotropic medications, and strategies for overcoming those barriers. Members' attendance at self-help meetings and their reactions to them are regularly reviewed. Although pre-AA groups are clearly distinguished from twelve-step meetings, some rituals, such as reading aloud from twelve-step books and closing meetings by holding hands and reciting a prayer together, are practiced in group to increase members' comfort with them and to stimulate discussion. The active treatment phase of this model is attending AA or other self-help meetings with sobriety as a goal. Members in this phase are encouraged to continue attending the pre-AA group to serve as mentors to their peers.

Several authors have described twelve-step self-help groups that specialize in serving a membership with dual disorders (Bricker, 1994; Hendrickson and Schmal, 1994). These include groups initiated by community AA volunteers (Kurtz and others, 1995; Woods, 1991) and groups initiated by professionals (Caldwell and White, 1991). The former follow a standard AA format but also include discussion of "recovery" from mental illness (Kurtz and others, 1995). The latter generally follow an AA format with some modifications, such as allowing professional involvement.

**Broad-Based Educational-Supportive Models.** This approach posits that change in substance abuse occurs because of education about the effects of substances and social support from others experiencing similar difficulties. An explicit educational curriculum is provided, interspersed with the sharing of personal experiences and open discussion of recent substance abuse. Other than a shared focus on education and engendering social support among group members, applications of this model vary widely in terms of their eligibility requirements, duration of treatment, and specific clinical methods employed (for example, psychoeducational techniques, skills training, and problem solving).

Some approaches limit participation in the group to persons who are motivated to reduce substance abuse (Hellerstein and Meehan, 1987; Hellerstein, Rosenthal, and Miner, 1995), whereas others do not (Alfs and McLellan, 1992; Sciacca, 1987; Straussman, 1985). The approach described by Hellerstein, Rosenthal, and Miner differs from others in that groups are offered on a time-unlimited basis. Common across the different educational-supportive group treatments is avoidance of direct confrontation, maintaining an affectively benign and supportive milieu, helping clients understand how substance abuse affects their psychiatric illness, and familiarizing clients with how AA-type groups in the community work. For example, in Sciacca's (1987) group, speakers from AA and Narcotics Anonymous (NA) are invited to describe their groups to members.

In general, the educational-supportive model is the least theoretically distinct model of integrated group treatment for dually diagnosed individuals. The approach is compatible with stagewise treatments without explicitly endorsing the stage model of recovery. For example, the approaches of Alfs and

McClellan (1992), Sciacca (1987), and Straussman (1985) resemble persuasion groups, whereas Hellerstein and Meehan's (1987) groups resemble active treatment groups (described below). Members are encouraged to try AA and other self-help groups, but the main purpose of educational-supportive groups is not to prepare clients for self-help groups in the community. Finally, although some skills training techniques may be used in some of these groups, they do not embrace a social-learning conceptualization of treating dual disorders.

**Social Skills Training.** Social skills training (SST) refers to a social learning approach to improving interpersonal competence through modeling, role playing, positive and corrective feedback, and homework assignments (Liberman, DeRisi, and Mueser, 1989). SST procedures have traditionally been used to teach interpersonal skills, but can also be used to teach self-care skills such as grooming and hygiene. Although SST methods are employed by other group models, the SST model differs in two respects. First, the SST model conceptualizes the needs of dually diagnosed persons in terms of skill deficits that interfere with the ability to develop a lifestyle free from substance abuse. Thus, deficits in areas such as the ability to resist offers to use substances, recreational skills, or skill in managing interpersonal conflicts are thought to contribute to substance abuse. Second, because the focus of SST is on teaching new skills or relearning old ones, an emphasis is placed on *explicit* modeling of skills and repeated behavioral rehearsals, guided by the principle that over-practice of skills is necessary to achieving mastery (Ericsson and Charness, 1994). In contrast, other group models are more likely to facilitate skill development by *implicit* use of modeling (for example, skills are used by leaders, but are not specifically demonstrated for participants) and talking about skills, with only occasional use of role plays and behaviorally based feedback.

In order to teach an array of specific skills to clients, SST models employ detailed, preplanned curricula and follow a specific agenda. Despite the structure of the groups, the SST approach places high value on fostering supportive relationships between group members, improving understanding about the effects of substances, and addressing the emergent needs of clients (Jerrell and Ridgely, 1995). As with other models, specific SST programs vary in their content, format, and structure. Nikkel (1994) has described a long-term SST program based on training modules developed by Liberman and others (1987), with skills taught in areas such as relationships, resisting offers to use substances, self-care, money management, sleep hygiene, leisure, and vocational and educational functioning. The group format and other formats (for example, family psychoeducation and individual therapy) are used to teach skills. Carey, Carey, and Meisler (1990) describe a skills training approach in which problem-solving skills are systematically taught to outpatients to enable them to more effectively manage stress and interpersonal situations. We have recently developed a time-limited inpatient SST group with a focus on teaching interpersonal skills, strategies for managing negative emotions, and alternative recreational activities (Mueser and others, 1995).

As with the educational-supportive group model, a key distinction between the social skills model and stagewise treatment is that the skills approach does not formally incorporate the distinction between persuasion and active treatment into the group. Similarly, skills training and other behavioral strategies are typically included in stagewise treatment (as indicated in the following section), as well as a range of other clinical methods. Consistent with the other group models, the SST model incorporates education into the curriculum and endorses the potential benefits of self-help groups such as AA (for example, Nikkel, 1994).

**Stagewise Treatment.** Stagewise treatment refers to group interventions designed to meet the unique needs of clients at different stages of recovery from substance abuse. Over the past several years, we have developed and implemented stagewise group treatments at different community mental health centers throughout New Hampshire (Noordsy and Fox, 1991). Although four different stages of recovery have been proposed, for the purposes of group treatment, clients in the second stage (persuasion) participate in one type of group (a *persuasion group*), and clients in the last two stages (active treatment and relapse prevention) participate in a second type of group (an *active treatment group*). Clients in the engagement phase may attend some persuasion groups, but regular attendance does not typically occur until they complete this stage.

The unique feature of this approach is recognition that many individuals with dual diagnoses lack motivation for treatment, and that motivation must be developed for treatment to succeed. This approach draws on the techniques of the other three group intervention models, using them as they are relevant for individuals within groups and subdividing their use across two motivational stages. Leaders must be skilled in the techniques of the other approaches to be able to use them when needed.

*Persuasion Groups.* By definition, clients in the engagement and persuasion stages of recovery do not recognize that they have a substance abuse problem, and do not endorse the goal of reducing substance use. Therefore the primary goal of persuasion groups is to develop clients' awareness of how substances complicate their lives. A combination of clinical strategies is employed to assist participants in examining the consequences of their substance use, including education and motivational interviewing techniques (Miller and Rollnick, 1991), such as empathic listening and helping clients perceive the discrepancy between their personal goals and substance use. Persuasion groups can be conducted either with inpatients (Kofoed and Keys, 1988) or outpatients (Noordsy and Fox, 1991). We provide below a brief description of how these groups are conducted on an outpatient basis at several community mental health centers in New Hampshire.

The optimal format for groups is to have two leaders, one with expertise in treating mental illness and the other with expertise in addictive disorders. Groups are held weekly, often shortly after the weekend so that periods of heavy substance use are likely to be fresh in clients' minds. Some groups run for 45–60 minutes, whereas others have two 20–30 minute sessions separated by a short break. Brief sessions reduce the intensity and enable clients with limited attention spans to participate. Groups are open to all clients and weekly attendance is encouraged but not required. Because initial attendance is usually a problem, the groups serve refreshments, include activities (for example, community trips and videos), and are extremely supportive. Clients need not acknowledge a problem with substances in order to attend and those who have been using substances are allowed to attend group if they behave appropriately.

Persuasion groups are not confrontational. They assume instead that recognition of a substance abuse problem occurs over time in the context of peer group support and education. The stated goal of the group is to help members learn more about the role that alcohol and drugs play in their lives. Group leaders provide didactic material on substances and mental illness, but they spend most of their effort facilitating peer interactions and feedback about substance use. Leaders actively limit the level of affect, monitor psychotic behaviors, and maintain the group's focus on substance abuse. Members who turn up at group inebriated are allowed to participate (if they are not disruptive), and members are permitted to leave early if they choose. Those who are reluctant to participate are invited to contribute at least once or twice during each meeting. The overriding theme is to encourage participation in the group and to gently, repeatedly expose members to opportunities to explore the reinforcing and destructive effects of their substance use.

Persuasion group sessions often begin with a review of each member's use of substances over the previous week. This discussion is nonjudgmental so that members feel safe in reporting their use honestly. As a member discusses a recent period of intoxication, others help to identify antecedents, including internal emotional states, and consequences of use. All members are encouraged to contribute to this process, perhaps offering advice or relating a similar experience. Leaders field questions and provide brief information on addiction, the effects of various substances on physical and mental health, and the interactions between drugs and medications. Relevant films, short readings, or group outings are occasionally used to stimulate interest and discussion if needed, although lengthy didactic presentations are avoided. Group members often ask leaders about their own use of substances. Leaders are typically open about their use; those who are recovering from addiction may share their own experiences, and those who are not honestly relate their past experimentation, subsequent consequences if any, and current choices, facilitating discussion of distinctions between use and abuse.

*Active Treatment Groups.* These groups are focused, behavioral, and aimed at reducing substance use and promoting abstinence. Members working toward a common goal of abstinence actively give each other feedback and support. Unlike persuasion groups, there is an assumption of sobriety during participation in active treatment groups. Although not required, members are encouraged to try out self-help meetings as a form of active treatment work or one route to sobriety. Members often accompany each other to meetings. The group work includes review of members' experiences using self-help and focuses on developing the skills to successfully negotiate a self-help program (at times similar to pre-AA groups).

Behavioral principles of addiction treatment (Monti, Abrams, Kadden, and Cooney, 1989) guide active treatment groups. This approach is less stimulating than some others and addresses the development of skills that dually diagnosed clients often lack. Members learn social skills through role plays and group interaction and use one another for support and assistance in attending self-help meetings. They are trained in assertiveness, giving and receiving criticism, drink or drug refusal skills, making new friends, and managing thoughts about alcohol or other drug use. Clients learn to develop constructive substitutes for substance use, to manage craving, difficult emotions, or symptoms. Another common focus of these groups is on learning coping strategies. For example, clients experiencing cravings for substances may be taught the use of imagery by transforming positive images for a desired substance into negative images, such as hangovers, psychotic relapses, or fights.

Clients also learn to recognize situations that increase their risk of substance use and to use relapse prevention techniques for managing these situations (Marlatt and Gordon, 1985). For example, relaxation training and principles of sleep hygiene are used to regain control over anxiety and insomnia that may lead to the use of substances. Many members need help with concrete situations such as learning how to set limits on substance-abusing friends. The cognitive and behavioral chain of events leading up to episodes of craving or substance use are identified and strategies for preventing future episodes are developed. Members are encouraged to write down their internal or interpersonal struggles during the week so that they can work on them in the group. Leaders help them discover and label strategies for managing emotional experiences that they had been obliterating with substance use and to appreciate the gradual improvements in their mental health and stability that come with sobriety. Members often gain a greater sense of responsibility for managing both of their illnesses during this process. When relapses do occur, group members offer support and help in developing plans to minimize the severity of the relapse in order to arrest the backslide to substance abuse and dependence.

*Combined Persuasion and Active Treatment Groups.* In some settings where persuasion and active treatment groups have been running for several years, it may be advantageous to combine the two formats into a single group. Despite the fact that all clients participate in the same group, intervention is tailored to the specific stage of recovery for each client. We provide several clinical vignettes illustrating stagewise treatment in a combined group.

## Clinical Vignettes

The following vignettes illustrate typical interactions at different stages of group development in the stagewise model.

**Beginning the Group.** The leaders start group by asking each member to describe their use of substances or craving for them over the past week. This exercise is used to provide continuity from group to group and to develop material for the session.

LEADER: Good morning. Let's go ahead and get started. How was your week, George?

GEORGE: I'm still drinking and smoking and I just can't stop. I'm awake half the night because I can't breathe, and I cough and hack my guts out every morning. I've got to stop. It's killing me.

LEADER: You've been struggling with this for a while. Would you like to develop a plan for quitting in group today? There's a lot of experience in this room that you could put to work for you.

GEORGE: Couldn't hurt.

LEADER: Good, we'll get back to that. How was your week, Jim?

JIM: This has been a pretty intense week for me. I didn't sleep much over the weekend and I got pretty manic.

LEADER: Were you using?

JIM: I haven't had a drink in three months. Drinking didn't have anything to do with how I was feeling this weekend. I was going through some intense personal exploration and my medications got all screwed up.

LEADER: You have often mentioned smoking pot to the group.

JIM: Well, sure I was smoking, but that had nothing to do with it. I smoke less when I'm manic because I don't need it as much.

LEADER: Would it be fair to look at that some more later?

JIM: Fair enough.

LEADER: How was your week, Brian?

BRIAN: Pretty lousy. I couldn't sleep good and I had pains in my neck and back and shoulders. I hurt all over.

LEADER: Were you using?

BRIAN: No, it's been a year since I've had a drink or a drug. I didn't want to wreck that, but I sure was thinking that a beer would help kill the pain.

**Developing a Plan to Quit.** George is a fifty-two-year-old divorced male with diagnoses of schizophrenia and alcohol dependence. His psychotic illness had onset in his mid-thirties and was characterized by frequent medication discontinuation and episodes of behaviorally disruptive psychosis. He has used alcohol heavily since his teens except for five years during his marriage when his wife disallowed it. During one severe episode of drinking and psychosis he stole a car in response to his delusions. He was convicted of auto theft and his probation required medication compliance and abstinence. Since the probation ended three years ago he has remained medication compliant and has not had another severe psychotic episode, but he returned to daily drinking. He attended the stagewise group regularly during his probation, but now drops out for a month or two at a time. He is in group for the first time in five weeks today. He has repeatedly identified an abstinence goal and made attempts at quitting drinking, placing him in the early active treatment stage.

LEADER: George, you mentioned a lot of problems related to smoking and drinking. Would you like some help figuring out how to change?

GEORGE: Well, I'm moving to a new place so I was thinking of quitting then. Is that what you mean?

LEADER: That's excellent. Starting in a new place would help to avoid craving being triggered by the reminders of using around your old home. Would you like to pick a quit date?

GEORGE: I'm going to be way out in the boonies. I just won't bring it with me and I won't go out to see anyone anymore. Everyone I know drinks and smokes, even my girlfriend. I've had enough of her. I wish someone would just lock me up in detox for a few weeks, but they don't do that anymore. I can't do it around my friends.

BILL: I wouldn't be alone. That'll drive you to drink.

MARY: Won't you get bored? I'd be pacing the floor thinking about using the whole time.

GEORGE: No, I like to be alone. When I quit before, nine years ago, I just went out in the woods for a few weeks and quit everything, even medication.

LEADER: How did that work out?

GEORGE: Well I ended up in the hospital, but I didn't drink for two years.

JIM: You don't want to end up back in there. Besides, you'll need to go to the store sometime and there's always beer there begging you to take it home. I think you should go to AA.

LEADER: Maybe we can develop a plan using the things that worked for you before and some of these other suggestions to help you get to your goal. One thing that might help is establishing a date and time now for starting your new healthy lifestyle. You are less likely to just keep using out of habit and miss the opportunity of using your move to help you if you make a clear plan for yourself.

GEORGE: Well, I'm moving this weekend.

LEADER: Would you like to be using during the move?

GEORGE: Yeah, I'll probably be drinking some that day. I'll be all in by Saturday night.

LEADER: Would you like to stop using then?

GEORGE: Yeah, that's it. I'll stop using Saturday night at, say six o'clock.

LEADER: What other things have helped people to get sober?

JIM: I needed to have people to talk to to get through it. Sober people. That's why I went to AA.

GEORGE: The guy I'm renting from is real nice and he doesn't drink or smoke. I can hang around with him. I guess I could try AA again. I went years ago on probation but it just made me want to drink more to hear all those stories.

LEADER: It might be worth trying AA again. You might hear those stories differently now that you want to quit. Could you use any family members for support?

GEORGE: They're all drunks too for the most part except for my sister. She quit about three years ago. She goes to AA actually.

JIM: You could talk to her for support and ask her to take you to a few meetings, too.

LEADER: Would the folks in this group be willing to help George out if he needed support?

JIM: Sure, call me anytime George. We could have coffee and talk.

MARY: I'd be happy to help out, but I don't have a phone. I still live in the same place.

BRIAN: Yeah, I'll help.

LEADER: I'll make sure your case manager knows about this plan so she can work with you on it, too. You know, Mary mentioned craving before. Maybe we can generate a list of things to do to get through a craving.

GEORGE: When I get craving a drink I can just taste it. It's hard to think of anything else. That's what gets me.

MARY: You could keep a list with you that tells you what to do.

LEADER: You know, Mary's right. It's hard to think when you are in the middle of a craving, but if you have a list handy you can just read it. Why don't each of us come up with a personal list of things to do to get through a craving. I'll pass around index cards and let's each write down ten things we could do to get through a craving and then we'll go around the room and share ideas. . . .

**Persuasion Work.** Jim is a thirty-five-year-old man with advanced degrees in philosophy who has been diagnosed with a bipolar affective disorder. He used alcohol and other drugs extensively throughout his postsecondary schooling and subsequent employment. He suffered a head injury in a car accident at age twenty-five and subsequently developed chronic bipolar symptoms with psychotic features exacerbated by severe alcoholism and marijuana abuse. Jim has attended stagewise treatment groups intermittently in the last two years. Initially he did persuasion stage work in group, recognized severe physical consequences of his alcohol use, and developed a goal of abstinence from alcohol. He developed active treatment plans in individual and group settings and used AA meetings as well. During this time his group participation became erratic, attending for several sessions after each relapse back to alcohol use and psychosis. After several state hospital admissions he reestablished an abstinence goal and has been attending group regularly for nine months. He had a brief, severe relapse to drinking three months ago and has been abstinent from alcohol since. He continues marijuana use. He is therefore doing relapse prevention work around alcohol, but still requires persuasion stage work focusing on his marijuana use.

LEADER: Jim, you mentioned that you had a rough weekend with some medication problems and mania, and you were smoking some too.

JIM: Nothing different from usual. Actually when I'm manic I smoke less; I don't need it as much. It's just that I cut back on the lithium for a little while and things got a little out of hand. I got pretty psychotic, but I just took some [chlorpromazine] and got back in control. I'm all set now.

LEADER: How much were you smoking?

JIM: Oh, you know, whenever I got the chance. Marijuana has been a really positive drug for me. I don't look at it as a drug for me any more than I would psychiatric medications. It's a tool that helps me have insights and understand life.

LEADER: Were you smoking any more than usual last week?

JIM: Well, I did get a good supply last week so you could say that I was smoking a fair amount until it ran out.

LEADER: When did it run out?

JIM: Friday night.

LEADER: When did you get psychotic?

JIM: I don't know. I guess it started Friday during the day.

LEADER: Do you like being psychotic?

JIM: It's interesting to a point but I don't like getting real paranoid. I usually quit smoking before it gets too bad.

LEADER: But you didn't this time. How come?

JIM: It was really good stuff and I had a lot of it. I guess I just didn't want to stop badly enough.

LEADER: What do you think, Brian?

BRIAN: I don't know. Sounds like he couldn't stop.

LEADER: George?

GEORGE: I know where he's coming from. It's hard to say no when it's right there under your nose.

LEADER: And you usually don't feel the consequences until it's too late. Jim, no one can decide what's right for you except yourself but it sounds like your pot use wasn't all that pleasurable this week.

JIM: Yeah, I was pretty hurting by the end.

LEADER: What did it cost you to buy?

JIM: Forty bucks.

LEADER: Was it worth it?

JIM: If you'd have asked me Thursday I would have said yes. I don't know now.

## Common and Unique Factors in Group Models

Different models of integrated group treatment share many common characteristics. All the approaches educate clients about the effects of substance use and avoid the confrontation typical of many programs for primary substance abuse. Each of the models strives to create a supportive social milieu within the group and encourages socialization between members outside of the group. All the models also recognize the role that psychiatric disorders play in increasing clients' risk to substance abuse (for example, symptoms, stigma, and lack of leisure activities) and attempt to address illness-related factors that may contribute to this vulnerability through education, skills training, and supportive techniques. Finally, all the models endorse the potential benefits of self-help organizations such as AA in aiding clients in their recovery from substance use disorders.

The models of group treatment can be distinguished primarily in their philosophy of recovery. By its very nature, only stagewise treatment explicitly identifies goals and targets interventions based on the client's stage of recovery and focuses on self-assessment of motivational development as a prerequisite to sobriety-oriented work. Twelve-step groups have a strong orientation toward recovery based on the traditional AA model and toward trying to engage clients in self-help groups available in the community. The skills training approach places a premium on the acquisition of new skills and downplays the possible role of insight in aiding recovery. Although none of these foci are unique to one model, their emphasis differs across the models. Thus the twelve-step, educational-supportive, stagewise, and social skills models are each based on somewhat different but compatible philosophies. Overall, the integrated approaches to group treatment have more in common than they are unique.

## Research on Group Treatment

Over the past decade a number of studies have examined the effectiveness of group treatment in the context of integrated programs for dually diagnosed persons. The results of these studies are summarized in Table 3.1. As can be seen from inspection of this table, research has been limited by the paucity of controlled studies, especially those involving random assignment to treatment groups. None of the three studies in which clients were randomly assigned to *group treatment* and *no group treatment* categories found an added effect for the group intervention (Carey, Carey, and Meisler, 1990; Hellerstein, Rosenthal, and Miner, 1995; Lehman, Herron, Schwartz, and Myers, 1993). These studies were limited, however, by the relatively brief intervention period (ranging from six weeks to one year), small sample sizes (ranging from twenty-nine to fifty-four), and nonattendance in the group condition (for example, Lehman, Herron, Schwartz, and Myers, 1993). Bond, McDonel, Miller, and Pensec's (1991) quasi-experimental study was unique in that clients who received group treatment over eighteen months improved more in substance abuse outcomes than clients who received either ACT or standard treatment. It is possible that nonrandom assignment of clients to treatment condition contributed to the differential outcome in substance abuse. Jerrell and Ridgely's (1995) study suggests that different approaches to integrated treatment produce similar results, with some advantage for the skills training model. By and large, however, the outcomes for the different integrated treatments in this study

**Table 3.1. Summary of Research on Group Treatment for Dually Diagnosed Clients**

| Investigator | Number of Clients | Treatment Groups | Duration of Treatment | Research Design | Outcomes |
|---|---|---|---|---|---|
| Kofoed and others (1986) | 32 | Educational-supportive | Up to 2 years (weekly sessions) | Pre-post | 35% of clients remained in treatment for more than 3 months. Clients who remained in treatment spent less time in hospital. |
| Hellerstein and Meehan (1987) | 10 | Educational-supportive | 1 year (weekly sessions) | Pre-post | 50% of clients remained in treatment 1 year. Clients who remained in treatment spent less time in hospital. |
| Kofoed and Keys (1988) | 109 | Stagewise (persuasion) | Inpatient-brief (2 sessions/wk.) | Non-experimental comparison of two | Clients in treatment group referred for outpatient substance abuse treatment more than clients who did not receive treatment group. |
| | 109 | No inpatient group treatment | | | No differences in rehospitalization over 6 months. |
| Carey and others (1990) | 17 | Social skills training (problem solving) | 6 weeks (2 sessions/wk.) | Random assignment to group/no group treatment | At 1 month follow-up, no difference in problem-solving skills between groups. |
| | 12 | No group treatment | | | |

**Table 3.1.** (continued)

| Investigator | Number of Clients | Treatment Groups | Duration of Treatment | Research Design | Outcomes |
|---|---|---|---|---|---|
| Bond and others (1991) | 23 | Educational-supportive | 18 months (variable group session frequency) | Quasi-experimental | Group treatment and ACT clients remained in treatment longer. |
| | 31 | Assertive community treatment (ACT) (no group treatment) | | | Group treatment clients had fewer hospitalizations; ACT clients spent less time in hospital. |
| | 43 | Control (no group treatment) | | | Group treatment clients used less alcohol and drugs. |
| | | | | | All clients improved in quality of life. |
| Noordsy and Fox (1991) | 18 | Stagewise | 3 years (weekly sessions) | Pre-post | Approximately 60% of all clients attained stable abstinence and 80% of group attenders. |
| Alfs and McClellan | 145 | Educational-supportive | 6–8 weeks (daily meetings in day hospital; weekly evening aftercare) | Pre-post | 66% clients completed program 33% of clients in active treatment relapsed. |
| Lehman and others (1993) | 29 | Educational-supportive and twelve-step and intensive case management | 1 year (daily sessions) | Random assignment to group/no group treatment. | Clients in group treatment attended 20% of the groups. |
| | 25 | Control (no group treatment) | | | No differences or changes in symptoms, substance abuse, or life satisfaction. |

| Study | N | Condition | Duration | Design | Findings |
|---|---|---|---|---|---|
| Hellerstein and others (1995) | 24 | Educational-supportive | 8 months (2 sessions/week) | Random assignment to group/no group treatment. | 36% of clients remained in treatment. Clients improved in substance abuse and symptoms, but no differences between group treatment and controls. |
| | 23 | Control (standard, non-integrated, no group treatment) | | | |
| Jerrell and Ridgely (1995) | 39 | Twelve-step | 18 months | Quasi-experimental | Clients improved on most measures of substance abuse, symptoms, social functioning, and service utilization. Clients in SST tended to do best, followed by CM, followed by 12-step. |
| | 45 | Case management (CM) and sporadic educational groups | | | |
| | 48 | Social skills training (SST) | | | |
| Drake and others (1996) | 158 | Integrated treatment and cognitive-behavioral groups | 18 months | Quasi-experimental | Clients in integrated treatment improved more in alcohol abuse, spent less time in hospitals, and had more stable housing. Clients in both treatments improved in symptoms and quality of life. |
| | 59 | Standard treatment with twelve-step groups | | | |

were similar. In a recently completed study, Drake and others (1996) reported that integrated substance abuse and mental health treatment, with a heavy reliance on cognitive-behavioral groups, resulted in better alcohol abuse and housing outcomes for homeless dually diagnosed persons than standard services that employed twelve-step groups. Similar to Jerrell and Ridgely's (1995) study, however, the two treatment conditions studied by Drake and others differed in a variety of respects other than the group models used, so it is difficult to ascribe differences in outcomes to the group models employed.

Although the experimental evidence supporting the added benefits of group treatment is meager, more naturalistic pre-post study designs suggest that group treatment, when provided with other elements of integrated treatment, is associated with improved outcomes compared to standard care. There is also a trend for integrated treatments that include groups to more successfully engage and retain clients in treatment, which is associated with better outcomes (Drake, McHugo, and Noordsy, 1993; Hellerstein and Meehan, 1987; Hellerstein, Rosenthal, and Miner, 1995; Kofoed and Keys, 1988; Kofoed, Kania, Walsh, and Atkinson, 1986). These findings are consistent with the positive results of the NIMH Community Support Program Demonstration Studies of Services for Young Adults with Severe Mental Illness and Substance Abuse (Mercer-McFadden and Drake, 1993), which examined the effects of integrated treatment, including group intervention, across thirteen different sites.

It appears that one obstacle to demonstrating the effects of group treatment is that integrated approaches are so powerful that it is difficult to show the added advantage of a single component of the model. At the same time, a systematic dismantling of the different components of integrated treatment models is a formidable task, both because of the sheer number of components (for example, case management, family intervention, group models, use of monitoring techniques, control over contingencies such as funds, housing, and hospitalization) and because of the variety of articulated integrated treatment models. An additional research problem is that only 50 to 75 percent of dually diagnosed clients will attend groups even minimally, and 30 to 50 percent regularly. Therefore the group must have very strong effects to exceed the "noise" of nonattenders.

## Recommendations for Future Research on Group Treatment

Significant progress has been made over the past decade in the treatment of dually diagnosed persons. Coincident with the recognition that these individuals need comprehensive interventions that simultaneously address both disorders, an understanding has developed that short-term treatments produce short-term benefits, and that long-term strategies are required for meaningful results to accrue. Group intervention has consistently been included as a vital component of integrated treatment programs, yet there are scant data to support this important role. In fact, only two controlled studies suggest added benefits of group treatment, and both included quasi-experimental, not fully randomized designs (Bond and others, 1991; Jerrell and Ridgley, 1995).

Several avenues of research may shed light on the effects of group treatment. First, there is a pressing need for more controlled research that compares the effects of integrated treatment *with* versus *without* group therapy. In order for such research to be meaningful, the treatments must be provided long-term (preferably at least eighteen months), the group model must be sufficiently specified, and a moderate proportion of the clients must attend the groups. Studies in which few clients regularly attend groups tell us little about the efficacy of group intervention (for example, Lehman, Herron, Schwartz, and Myers, 1993). It may be fruitful to identify characteristics of clients most likely to attend treatment groups so that research on the efficacy of group treatment can focus primarily on these clients, and clinicians can explore strategies for increasing attendance at groups.

Second, there is a need to examine whether specific client attributes are predictive of clinical response to group treatment in general or to specific models of group intervention. For example, it might be argued that social skills deficits will predict a better response to social skills training, an external locus of control will be related to improvements in a twelve-step approach, whereas antisocial personality characteristics predict a poor response to all group interventions. Although such correlational research is necessarily speculative, it can form the basis for hypothesis generation that can be subsequently evaluated in experimental designs.

Finally, research into group treatment may provide valuable insights into the relationship between specific dimensions of client participation in the group (for example, level of participation and specific content of verbal contributions) and their current and future clinical functioning. At present, there is little available information to aid clinicians in understanding when and for whom the group intervention is working. Research on client group behavior and patterns of substance abuse may assist clinicians in identifying clients who are ready to begin tapering their substance use, who are at increased risk for relapse, or who may be on the verge of dropping out. Such information would enable clinicians to take proactive steps to enhance outcomes.

Substantial advances have been made in treating this difficult population. The positive effects of many different interventions that have included a group treatment component bode well for the efficacy of this modality. Despite this, the benefits of group treatment remain to be empirically demonstrated. The recent specification of a number of coherent group treatment models poises the field to address this important question.

## References

Alfs, D. S., and McClellan, T. A. "A Day Hospital Program for Dual Diagnosis Patients in a VA Medical Center." *Hospital and Community Psychiatry,* 1992, *43,* 241–244.

Bartels, S. J., and Thomas, W. N. "Lessons from a Pilot Residential Treatment Program for People with Dual Disorders of Severe Mental Illness and Substance Use Disorder." *Psychosocial Rehabilitation Journal,* 1991, *15,* 19–30.

Bond, G., McDonel, E. C., Miller, L. D., and Pensec, M. "Assertive Community Treatment and Reference Groups: An Evaluation of their Effectiveness for Young Adults with Serious Mental Illness and Substance Use Problems." *Psychosocial Rehabilitation Journal,* 1991, *15,* 31–43.

Bricker, M. "The Evolution of Mutual Help Groups for Dual Recovery." *TIE-Lines,* 1994, *11,* 1–4.

Caldwell, S., and White, K. K. "Co-Creating a Self-Help Recovery Movement." *Psychosocial Rehabilitation Journal,* 1991, *15,* 91–95.

Carey, M. P., Carey, K. B., and Meisler, A. W. "Training Mentally Ill Chemical Abusers in Social Problem Solving." *Behavior Therapy,* 1990, *21,* 511–518.

Dixon, L., Haas, G., Weiden, P., Sweeney, J., and Frances, A. "Drug Abuse in Schizophrenic Patients: Clinical Correlates and Reasons for Use." *American Journal of Psychiatry,* 1991, *148,* 224–230.

Drake, R. E., Bartels, S. B., Teague, G. B., Noordsy, D. L., and Clark, R. E. "Treatment of Substance Abuse in Severely Mentally Ill Patients." *Journal of Nervous and Mental Disease,* 1993, *181,* 606–611.

Drake, R. E., McHugo, G. J., and Noordsy, D. L. "Treatment of Alcoholism Among Schizophrenic Outpatients: Four-Year Outcomes." *American Journal of Psychiatry,* 1993, *150,* 328–329.

Drake, R. E., Yovetich, N. A., Bebout, R. R., Harris, M., and McHugo, G. J. "Integrated Treatment for Dually Diagnosed Homeless Adults." Unpublished manuscript, 1996

Ericsson, K. A., and Charness, N. "Expert Performance: Its Structure and Acquisition." *American Psychologist,* 1994, *49,* 725–747.

Hellerstein, D. J., and Meehan, B. "Outpatient Group Therapy for Schizophrenic Substance Abusers." *American Journal of Psychiatry,* 1987, *144,* 1337–1339.

Hellerstein, D. J., Rosenthal, R. N., and Miner, C. R. "A Prospective Study of Integrated Outpatient Treatment for Substance-Abusing Schizophrenic Patients." *American Journal on Addictions,* 1995, *4,* 33–42.

Hendrickson, E., and Schmal, M. "Dual Disorder." *TIE-Lines,* 1994, *11,* 10–11.

Jerrell, J. M., and Ridgely, M. S. "Comparative Effectiveness of Three Approaches to Serving People with Severe Mental Illness and Substance Abuse Disorders." *Journal of Nervous and Mental Disease,* 1995, *183,* 566–576.

Kofoed, L. L., Kania, J., Walsh, T., and Atkinson, R. M. "Outpatient Treatment of Patients with Substance Abuse and Coexisting Psychiatric Disorders." *American Journal of Psychiatry,* 1986, *143,* 867–872.

Kofoed, L. L., and Keys, A. "Using Group Therapy to Persuade Dual-Diagnosis Patients to Seek Substance Abuse Treatment." *Hospital and Community Psychiatry,* 1988, *39,* 1209–1211.

Kurtz, L. F., Garvin, C. D., Hill, E. M., Pollio, D., McPherson, S., and Powell, T. J. "Involvement in Alcoholics Anonymous by Persons with Dual Disorders." *Alcoholism Treatment Quarterly,* 1995, *12,* 1–18.

Lehman, A. F., Herron, J. D., Schwartz, R. P., and Myers, C. P. "Rehabilitation for Adults with Severe Mental Illness and Substance Use Disorders: A Clinical Trial." *Journal of Nervous and Mental Disease,* 1993, *181,* 86–90.

Liberman, R. P., DeRisi, W. J., and Mueser, K. T. *Social Skills Training for Psychiatric Patients.* Needham Heights, Mass.: Allyn & Bacon, 1989.

Liberman, R., and Associates. *Psychiatric Rehabilitation of the Chronic Mental Patient.* Washington, D.C.: American Psychiatric Press, 1987.

Marlatt, G. A., and Gordon, J. R. *Relapse Prevention Maintenance Strategies in the Treatment of Addictive Behaviors.* New York: Guilford Press, 1985.

Mercer-McFadden, C., and Drake, R. E. *A Review of NIMH Demonstration Programs for Young Adults with Co-Occurring Severe Mental Illness and Substance Use Disorder.* Center for Community Mental Health Services, SAMSHA. Rockville, Md.: U.S. Department of Health and Human Services, 1993.

Miller, W. R., and Rollnick, S. *Motivational Interviewing: Preparing People to Change Addictive Behavior.* New York: Guilford Press, 1991.

Minkoff, K. "An Integrated Treatment Model for Dual Diagnosis of Psychosis and Addiction." *Hospital and Community Psychiatry,* 1989, *40,* 1031–1036.

Monti, P. M., Abrams, D. B., Kadden, R. M., and Cooney, N. L. *Treating Alcohol Dependence.* New York: Guilford Press, 1989.

Mueser, K. T., Fox, M., Kenison, L. B., and Geltz, B. L. *The Better Living Skills Group.* Treatment manual, 1995. Available from New Hampshire-Dartmouth Psychiatric Research, Main Building, 105 Pleasant St., Concord, NH, 03301.

Nikkel, R. E. "Areas of Skills Training for Persons with Mental Illness and Substance Use Disorders: Building Skills for Successful Living." *Community Mental Health Journal,* 1994, *30,* 61–72.

Noordsy, D. L., and Fox, L. "Group Intervention Techniques for People with Dual Disorders." *Psychosocial Rehabilitation Journal,* 1991, *15,* 67–78.

Noordsy, D. L., Schwab, B., Fox, L., and Drake, R. E. "The Role of Self-Help Programs in the Rehabilitation of Persons with Severe Mental Illness." *Community Mental Health Journal,* 1996, *32,* 71–78.

Prochaska, J. O., Velicer, W. F., DiClemente, C. C., and Fava, J. "Measuring Processes of Change: Application to the Cessation of Smoking." *Journal of Consulting and Clinical Psychology,* 1988, *56,* 520–528.

Sciacca, K. "New Initiatives on the Treatment of the Chronic Patient with Alcohol/Substance Use Problems." *TIE-Lines,* 1987, *4,* 5–6.

Straussman, J. "Dealing with Double Disabilities: Alcohol Use in the Club." *Psychosocial Rehabilitation Journal,* 1985, *8,* 8–14.

Test, M. A., Wallisch, L., Allness, D. J., and Ripp, K. "Substance Use in Young Adults with Schizophrenic Disorders." *Schizophrenia Bulletin,* 1989, *15,* 465–476.

Woods, J. D. "Incorporating Services for Chemical Dependency Problems into Clubhouse Model Programs: A Description of Two Programs." *Psychosocial Rehabilitation Journal,* 1991, *15,* 107–112.

KIM T. MUESER, Ph.D., is associate professor of psychiatry and community and family medicine at Dartmouth Medical School and a senior researcher at the New Hampshire–Dartmouth Psychiatric Research Center.

DOUGLAS L. NOORDSY, M.D., is assistant professor of psychiatry at Dartmouth Medical School and a research psychiatrist at the New Hampshire–Dartmouth Psychiatric Research Center.

*Homelessness is a far too common outcome for persons with dual diagnoses. This chapter discusses existing housing barriers and suggests housing, treatment, and support services responsive to population need.*

# Housing for Persons with Co-Occurring Mental and Addictive Disorders

*Fred C. Osher, Lisa B. Dixon*

## Case Example

Ms. B is a thirty-five-year-old Caucasian woman with a long history of frequent psychiatric hospitalization beginning at age seventeen. She has a diagnosis of schizophrenia (paranoid type) and at referral met criteria for binge-pattern alcohol dependence. Her drinking was associated with impulsive outbursts of violence, both toward herself and others. When not drinking, she was child-like and friendly although persistently paranoid about the efforts of others to "poison her." She had been living in the streets and in the shelter system of a large urban city for ten years prior to referral to an assertive community treatment (ACT) team that targeted homeless persons with severe mental illnesses. After a six-month period of outreach and regular meetings at a local diner, she seemed increasingly comfortable with several members of the case management team and agreed to a low dose of antipsychotic medication that she took irregularly. She initially refused to discuss her alcohol use, stating "it's none of your business." Over the six months, she acknowledged that she drank but vehemently denied that this alcohol use created any problems for her. At this point, she agreed to live in a transitional shelter that prohibited any substance use and provided on-site AA and NA group meetings. The ACT team was able to convince the shelter staff to waive their program requirement that all residents attend daily self-help meetings for Ms. B because of her behavior in groups. The team assured the shelter staff that alcohol abuse would be addressed in individual meetings with Ms. B. She did not drink for almost three months while living at this shelter. During this time, the ACT team assisted her in obtaining social security disability benefits; the team was named as the representative payee for this income support. She was assisted in finding her own apartment and being sober enabled her to gain access to housing subsidies. Although the team ensured that Ms. B's rent and bills were paid, she would sometimes use the leftover funds to buy alcohol, which induced bizarre behavior. When her landlord threatened eviction because of a behavioral disturbance, the ACT team would intervene by coming into the apartment to provide crisis counseling. These binging episodes became less frequent. Ms. B slowly became willing to acknowledge that alcohol use was not in her best interest and agreed to try group educational meetings about alcohol. She became increasingly attached to her apartment and stated that she did not want to do anything that might lead to her becoming homeless again. The team used this information to gently persuade her to examine the likely consequences of ongoing alcohol abuse and over time her drinking episodes disappeared entirely. Ms. B's compliance with medication improved somewhat but she remains suspicious and slightly paranoid.

## Dual Diagnosis and Unstable Housing

Access to appropriate housing is a critical component of care for persons with co-occurring mental and addictive disorders. Homelessness and housing instability can exacerbate addiction and mental illness, creating a malignant cycle of increased symptomatology, disability, and exposure to harsh living environments. Studies focusing on persons with dual diagnoses have shown that they are disproportionately at risk for housing instability and homelessness (Belcher, 1989; Drake, Osher, and Wallach, 1991). Epidemiologic studies have revealed that roughly 10 to 20 percent of homeless persons suffer from severe mental illnesses and co-occurring addictions (Tessler and Dennis, 1989; Drake, Osher, and Wallach, 1991). Furthermore, the majority of persons with co-occurring disorders never receive any mental or addictive treatment services (Kessler and others, 1994).

An aftercare study of patients of an urban state hospital revealed that over one-fourth of all patients and over one-half of patients with dual diagnoses had unstable housing and were at least temporarily homeless during the six months following discharge (Drake, Wallach, and Hoffman, 1989). Another study of discharged state hospital patients found that 36 percent of patients experienced homelessness within six months of their discharge (Belcher, 1989) and patients who used alcohol or other drugs were more likely to be in the homeless group. When homeless men with mental illness were followed from shelters to community housing, 44 percent returned to homelessness within eighteen months and co-occurring substance use disorders significantly increased the risk for homelessness (Caton and others, 1993). Drake and others (1991) found that this phenomenon is not restricted to urban locations. They studied housing instability of patients with schizophrenia in a rural area where patients had extensive family supports and low-cost housing was available. Their study found that co-occurring disorders were strongly correlated with housing instability and that the majority of patients with schizophrenia and alcohol problems experienced housing instability during a six-month period.

Thus alcohol and drug abuse by persons with severe mental illness must be considered a high-risk behavior for homelessness. In fact, a cohort of five investigators funded under the Stewart B. McKinney Homeless Assistance Act cited co-occurring substance use disorder as the major clinical factor associated with prolonged and repeated homeless episodes among homeless persons with severe mental illnesses (Center for Mental Health Services, 1994). Effective treatment of co-occurring disorders is critical to enabling an individual to escape cycles of homelessness. Conversely, effective interventions should reduce the risk of homelessness for those dually diagnosed persons currently in housing.

## Reasons for Dual Diagnosis–Homeless Relationship

Consideration of systemic, legal, and clinical perspectives facilitates understanding of why persons with dual diagnoses are at risk for housing instability and homelessness. Although research on all aspects of these issues has not been conducted, these issues merit consideration in developing residential and treatment services for dually diagnosed individuals.

**Systemic Issues.** Systemic barriers to services for persons with dual diagnoses have been well documented. Lack of a common administrative structure for alcohol, drug, and mental health services at the federal, state, and local levels; insufficient resources; historic distrust and philosophical conflicts between providers of addiction services and mental health services; and separate funding streams for treatment of both disorders have contributed to these barriers (Ridgely, Goldman, and Willenbring, 1990). Rapidly evolving health care reform initiatives that limit access to or funding for psychiatric or substance abuse services are likely to compound these barriers by failing to recognize, or respond to, the complex service needs of dually diagnosed individuals.

As a result of administrative divisions, many residential treatment programs for persons with mental illness specifically bar patients with co-occurring substance abuse problems. If they admit them, they may evict them after an episode of use. Residential addiction programs similarly bar patients with co-occurring mental illnesses, often identified as those who use prescribed psychopharmacologic medications. Clients encountering these bureaucratic barriers may experience frustration and anger or may accept the inaccessibility of the system as further justification for continued maladaptive behavior and hopelessness. The locus of responsibility for providing housing and clinical services to homeless persons with dual diagnoses is unclear and variable in different communities. The lack of clarity about whether mental health providers, substance abuse providers, or providers of housing services are responsible for assuring access to housing perpetuates the existence of housing gaps.

**Legal Issues.** Legal issues present obstacles to housing for persons with dual diagnoses. The Fair Housing Amendments Act of 1988 extended protection of federal fair housing legislation to persons with disabilities, including persons with mental illness. The full impact of this act in protecting against discriminatory housing practices remains to be seen (Petrila, 1995). In practice, however, persons with dual diagnoses face discriminatory treatment. Individuals with histories of drug dependence are not eligible for public housing programs unless they are receiving addiction treatment (Rubenstein, 1989) that is often in short supply with long waiting lists. Thus persons with mental illnesses may be shut out of the housing programs established for their care because of disabilities associated with drug or alcohol use. In addition, potential landlords may reject persons involved with illicit drugs because of perceived liability issues (Drake, Osher, and Wallach, 1991).

Criminal records and sometimes even contact with the criminal justice system can be a barrier to housing access. Homeless persons with dual diagnoses have been shown to have greater histories of arrest when compared to homeless persons without dual diagnoses. These arrests are frequently for misdemeanors caused by bizarre symptoms and erratic behavior, publicly displayed because of their lack of shelter (Abram and Teplin, 1991). Once they have an arrest record, it may be more difficult for persons with dual diagnoses to obtain housing of any kind.

In 1994 Congress passed legislation that limits the duration of income supports and entitlements to anyone whose disability is related to a substance use disorder to thirty-six months. Although it is too early to measure the effects of this legislation, one can hypothesize that increasing numbers of persons with addictive disorders, including those with dual diagnoses, will be unable to afford even the cheapest of accommodations. These legal issues serve as examples of how housing instability of persons with dual diagnoses can be an epiphenomenon of social policy rather than a clinical correlate.

**Clinical Issues.** Persons with dual diagnoses have been found to have greater rates of psychiatric symptoms (Negrete, Knapp, Douglas, and Smith, 1986; Drake and Wallach, 1989), noncompliance with treatment (Osher and others, 1994), psychiatric hospitalizations and use of emergency services (Safer, 1987; Bartels and others, 1993), and violent, disruptive behavior (Safer, 1987; Abram and Teplin, 1991)—including suicide (Drake, Osher, and Wallach, 1989; Dassori, Mezzich, and Keshavan, 1990; Bartels, Drake, and McHugo, 1992)—than persons with mental illnesses only. It is not surprising, then, that individuals with this clinical profile have trouble accessing housing and are at risk for losing housing.

Families already under stress from years of coping with mental illness may be unable to tolerate the additional disruption—and perhaps danger—associated with co-occurring substance abuse, resulting in eviction from the family home (Robinson, Dixon, Stewart, Harold, and Lehman, 1993). Providers in other residential settings such as board and care homes or public housing settings may also evict persons with dual diagnoses because they are unable to tolerate their erratic behaviors, their disturbance of other tenants, or their unreliable rental payments. Frequent or prolonged hospitalizations may result in loss of housing placement, particularly in locations where affordable housing is scarce and waiting lists are common.

Another important consideration is that persons with dual diagnoses may be unable to manage income or benefits, particularly if such funds are diverted to support a drug or alcohol habit. Consequently when no money for rent and other bills is available, streets, hospitals, or prisons become the only other shelter alternatives. The use of a representative payee, which can ameliorate this problem, is currently required for persons disabled as a result of a substance use disorder receiving social security income. Unfortunately, even if the need for a representative payee is obvious, it can be extremely difficult to find persons willing to serve as payees for these dually diagnosed individuals.

## Clinical Strategies That Facilitate Stable Housing

In order to treat dually diagnosed persons who are homeless or who are at risk for homelessness, clinicians must have an adequate understanding of the basic principles of treating persons with dual diagnoses. The heterogeneity of the dually diagnosed population with regard to both disabilities associated with their mental and addictive disorders and to their demographic, socioeconomic, and cultural backgrounds makes it incumbent on clinicians to design individualized treatment strategies. Distinguishing between substance abuse and dependence in persons with serious mental illnesses, for example, may govern the intensity of early treatment interventions (Bartels, Drake, and Wallach, 1995). Others have suggested that tailoring interventions to the unique needs of dually diagnosed women should be considered (Alexander, 1996).

As discussed by Carey (this volume), an integrated treatment program for dually diagnosed individuals organized around treatment phases—engagement, persuasion, active treatment, and relapse prevention (Osher and Kofoed, 1989)—has gained widespread acceptance. Successful programs have recognized the need to attend to both disorders, persisting through multiple crises and relapses, utilizing educational and supportive groups, and in many cases providing comprehensive case management services (Drake and Noordsy, 1994). Integrating motivational interventions matched to these stages is currently being investigated (Ziedonis and Fisher, 1994). Specific effects of these and other model interventions on housing stability remain to be studied. Clinical strategies to stabilize housing for persons with dual diagnoses will be discussed in terms of the treatment phases mentioned above.

**Engagement.** Housing instability and homelessness complicate the already difficult engagement phase in the treatment of individuals with co-occurring mental and addictive disorders. Assertive and prolonged outreach is essential because clients in this phase generally do not come to the program office or keep appointments. Lack of money for transportation, the daily demands of obtaining food and shelter, psychiatric symptoms, ongoing substance use, and associated organic deficits may cause clients to miss appointments. This can be a critical problem in efforts to secure limited housing resources such as Section 8 certificates (Dixon, Krauss, Myers, and Lehman, 1994). Because clients often have limited access to phones and mail, tracking clients requires tenacity as well as extensive contacts with providers in the community.

Providing for basic needs such as clothes, showers, and food may be helpful in the engagement process. Provision of badly needed material resources can help to draw clients into a trusting relationship in which staff can persuade them to enter treatment for substance abuse or mental illness and help them identify other long-term goals. The promise of safe, clean housing may motivate clients to enter the treatment system (Gaffney and Dixon, 1995). A treatment team must be able to access diverse housing or shelter options on an acute basis. Because housing instability persists even after housing is obtained, provision of on-site support is usually required. The capacity for crisis intervention for persons with dual diagnoses is critical. Crises, whether they are psychiatric, medical, or housing-related, may provide important opportunities to engage clients by addressing their acute needs.

Assessment of homeless individuals with dual diagnoses must begin in the engagement phase and continue longitudinally. Homeless persons with co-occurring disorders frequently avoid treatment; they may be suspicious of providers and unwilling to provide much personal information. They may also try to hide their substance use pattern for fear that disclosure may restrict their access to housing (Goldfinger and others, in press).

**Persuasion.** Persuasion involves reducing a patient's denial about a mental illness or substance abuse problem. Progress can be measured by a patient's acknowledgment that a problem exists and by the commitment to pursue active treatment. In addition to the persuasion strategies for dually diagnosed clients mentioned elsewhere in this volume, the link between housing opportunities and abstinence should be emphasized. How substance use has influenced housing arrangements in the past should be examined and, if appropriate, how access to current housing options is limited by ongoing drug use should be pointed out. Developing a discrepancy between the housing that the client hopes to obtain or maintain and the obstacles to this goal created by their ongoing drug abuse can be a key to persuading the individual to consider abstinence.

The use of representative payeeship assumes special importance in working with dually diagnosed homeless persons in the persuasion phase. Implicit in the condition of homelessness is that the client's basic needs are not being met. Although there may be a multitude of reasons for this (for example, the absence of decent affordable housing), the only way to stop the cycle of homelessness and drug use may be for the program, family, or some other individual to assume the responsibility of managing the person's finances. Stable housing requires stable finances. If a patient relapses and requires hospitalization and detoxification or simply spends some time on the streets, there can at least be a home to which he or she can return if the rent is paid. The implementation of a representative payee system fits well with the goals of the persuasion phase; it may alienate individuals during the engagement phase and may be a necessary condition for active treatment to proceed.

Related to the use of a representative payee is the use of other strategies that patients may perceive as coercive. The frequent legal entanglements of dually diagnosed persons offer opportunities for clinicians to use the requirement for court-ordered treatment. The clinician's attitude and approach in using coercion are critical. There is clearly an obligation to honor court-ordered requirements; additionally, concrete contingencies with direct consequences for failure to meet these conditions may be an important way to persuade people to begin treatment. Coercive approaches are *not* substitutes for treatment but may be an important component of an overall treatment strategy. Future research may reveal the extent to which structure and rules are themselves therapeutic at different phases of treating persons with dual diagnoses.

**Active Treatment.**  In the active treatment phase, patients develop the skills and relationships necessary to achieve and maintain sobriety and minimize disabilities associated with their mental illness. The basic strategies useful in this phase are discussed elsewhere in this volume (Carey, Chapter Two) and include individual and group therapies, education, and psychosocial rehabilitation. During this phase, the client's housing status should be reviewed and environmental or situational threats (living in a heavy drug trafficking zone, for example) to attaining abstinence should be identified.

**Relapse Prevention.**  Both addictions and mental illnesses tend to be relapsing disorders. The relapse prevention phase focuses on minimizing the extent of and damage caused by a patient relapse. The lack of social and family supports of the homeless individual with dual diagnoses may lead to increased fragility and greater vulnerability to relapse, both in terms of addiction and mental illness. Unanticipated relapses can lead to another episode of homelessness. It is thus especially important for programs and clinicians to plan contingencies if relapses occur to minimize the risk of repeated homelessness.

## Housing Strategies to Facilitate Recovery

Housing strategies for homeless or marginally-housed persons with dual diagnoses must be developed in tandem with clinical strategies. Development of housing strategies requires consideration of types of housing, associated support, organization, and funding. Newman (1992) describes two different philosophies that have been organizing principles of housing programs for severely and persistently mentally ill persons. The first, more traditional program uses a *level of care,* or *continuum* approach. The varying needs of the heterogeneous mentally ill population are addressed by offering several settings, each with different levels of service and supervision as well as restrictiveness. In this model, treatment and housing are linked. A second model has been called the *supported housing* model. In this model, the intensity of supported services varies with client need and the residential site remains the same (Ridgeway and Zipple, 1990; Harp, 1990).

Although some view these models as mutually exclusive, the authors and others believe that supported housing is simply another important part of the continuum of residential housing. The objective of housing diversity is to optimize choice, maintain community tenure, and ultimately to improve effectiveness (Fields, 1990; Kline, Harris, Bebout, and Drake, 1991). For persons with dual diagnoses, housing choice will be determined by community alternatives. This selection should be made by an assessment of the clinical needs and personal preferences of the individual. Housing selection may vary depending on what phase of treatment the person is in and what support needs exist. In addition to factors important to the housing choice of any citizen such as location, costs, and convenience, housing for dually diagnosed individuals requires the following special considerations.

**Residential Tolerance.** A critical question for persons with dual diagnoses is whether treatment can or should be separated from housing. Residential options must include settings that will tolerate the lengthy adjustment process required to feel safe and simultaneously struggle to control two disabling disorders. Kline, Harris, Bebout, and Drake argue (1991) that "transitions necessitated by administrative factors such as arbitrary time constraints, rather than by clinical needs, should be avoided."

The arguments to separate housing from treatment can lead to practical clinical problems. So-called *wet housing,* or housing in which the use of drugs and alcohol is tolerated, may be the only housing choice acceptable to the client in the early phases of engagement and treatment. Yet some clinicians believe that allowing substance use in housing sustains or enables use and is countertherapeutic. At the same time, the achievement and maintenance of sobriety may be unlikely, if not impossible, without adequate housing (Drake, Osher, and Wallach, 1991). Some patients may be motivated to stop using drugs if they are aware that their housing depends on their sobriety. Other patients will continue to use despite prohibitions, will get evicted, and will wind up on the streets in circumstances that are not conducive to pursuing sobriety. The solution to this dilemma is vexing and will require experimentation with different models and client choices.

At the present time, most housing options sponsored by mental health or substance abuse providers are *dry housing,* or housing in which alcohol and drug use is prohibited. Perhaps a housing continuum should provide for degrees of dryness, including *damp housing,* where there is an expectation of abstinence on the premises but clients are not required to agree to be abstinent off-site. At one end of the housing continuum could be shelters and other safe havens that are very tolerant of use, whereas toward the other end of the continuum there could be stronger expectations and limits. In a housing demonstration in which homeless persons were empowered to make house rules, alcohol was initially allowed on-site but later banned by the residents as they became aware of its destabilizing influence (Center for Mental Health Services, 1994).

The engagement phase might require flexible housing regulations while intensive and assertive support services are provided. High levels of structure and supervision may be unacceptable to persons during engagement. Once engagement is achieved, however, clients might tolerate a greater degree of structure and supervision during the persuasion and active treatment phases when peer interaction and clear limits may be therapeutic. Less structure and supervision consistent with supported housing models may be more appropriate during later phases of treatment such as the relapse prevention phase. The duration of on-site residential care remains a critical question for future investigations.

Safety. As mentioned above, homeless individuals are frequently victims of crime, and life on the streets is wrought with danger. Consideration of this fact is essential in planning housing for persons with mental illness who have drug addiction problems. Housing must be safe, whether it is a transitional shelter with a time-limited stay, a group home with other residents with mental illness, or an independent apartment fully integrated into the community.

Client Preference. In making choices about housing, programs must balance housing availability, client preferences, and client needs. Schutt and Goldfinger (1996) have found that although most people prefer independent housing, they do not always succeed at this choice. Clients with active addiction problems may prefer independent living but may have previous experience that suggests that they need more structure and supervision. Dixon, Krauss, Myers, and Lehman (1994) have shown that it was possible to honor the housing preferences of the majority of homeless mentally ill patients treated in their program that had a limited number of Section 8 certificates.

Shelterization. Unique to the long-term homeless individual is the phenomenon of *shelterization*. This refers to a process of acculturation and adaptation that homeless persons who use shelters may experience (Gounis and Susser, 1990; Grunberg and Eagle, 1990). Although it helps homeless persons cope with their surroundings in the short term, this process may impede the process of moving out of the shelter system that becomes a social community with familiar social rules. Some formerly homeless clients may experience loneliness when they make the transition from the noisy, busy shelter system to independent housing. There is some evidence that more intensive support during the transition from shelter to housing may result in increased residential stability (Center for Mental Health Services, 1994). If programs attend to these issues as well as clinical needs, housing stability should be enhanced.

Cooperative Agreements Between Providers and Housers. Given the complex and varied requirements of providing housing and clinical care as well as the historic administrative and economic separation of housing and treatment services, mental health, substance abuse, and housing providers should all agree prospectively to work together. Otherwise there is considerable danger that patients will fall between the cracks, receiving housing without mental health and addiction services or vice versa. Cooperative agreements should outline the respective roles and responsibilities of housing providers, mental health providers, and substance abuse providers. The specific details of such an agreement will need to reflect community resources. The common goal will be to maintain individuals with dual diagnoses in the community.

## Conclusion

Hypotheses about the optimal degree of structure, supervision, and support in housing for dually diagnosed persons await future research. Evaluators of the Robert Wood Johnson Foundation HUD Demonstration Program on Chronic Mental Illness noted, "It is particularly difficult to serve active substance abusers and those with recent histories of destructive behaviors using an independent housing strategy" (Newman, 1992). Inclusiveness has been advocated (Kline and others, 1991) as a principle of program development in which the goal is to provide services to as diverse a set of people as possible.

Although models for providing housing to individuals with co-occurring disorders have not been fully explicated and evaluated, reducing the morbidity and mortality associated with homelessness for these persons is critical. Dually diagnosed persons who are homeless or at risk for homelessness have special needs and characteristics that must be considered in treatment planning. Common principles must guide approaches to this population until empirical data are available. These include the following guidelines: individualized housing and treatment planning must be derived from thorough assessments, flexibility and creativity must outweigh intolerance and categorical programs, and ongoing therapeutic relationships must be established over time.

## References

Alexander, M. J. "Women with Co-Occurring Addictive and Mental Disorders: An Emerging Profile of Vulnerability." *American Journal of Orthopsychiatry,* 1996, *66* (1), 61–70.

Abram, K. M., and Teplin, L. A. "Co-Occurring Disorders Among Mentally Ill Jail Detainees." *American Psychologist,* 1991, *46,* 1036–1045.

Bartels, S. J., Drake, R. E., and McHugo, G. J. "Alcohol Use, Depression, and Suicide in Schizophrenia." *American Journal of Psychiatry,* 1992, *149,* 394–395.

Bartels, S. J., Drake, R. E., and Wallach, M. A. "Long-Term Course of Substance Use Disorders Among Patients with Severe Mental Illness." *Psychiatric Services,* 1995, *46* (3), 248–251.

Bartels, S. J., Teague, G. B., Drake, R. E., Clark, R. E., Bush, P., and Noordsy, D. L. "Substance Use in Schizophrenia: Service Utilization and Costs." *Journal of Nervous and Mental Disease,* 1993, *181,* 227–232.

Belcher, J. R. "On Becoming Homeless: A Study of Chronically Mentally Ill Persons." *Journal of Community Psychology,* 1989, *17,* 173–185.

Caton, C. L., Wyatt, R., Felix, A., Grunberg, J., and Dominquez, B. "Follow-Up of Chronically Homeless Mentally Ill Men." *American Journal of Psychiatry,* 1993, *150* (11), 1639–1642.

Center for Mental Health Services. *Making a Difference: Interim Status Report of the McKinney Research Demonstration Program for Homeless Mentally Ill Adults.* Rockville, Md.: Center for Mental Health Services, Substance Abuse and Mental Health Services Administration, 1994.

Dassori, A. M., Mezzich, J. E., and Keshavan, M. "Suicidal Indicators in Schizophrenia." *Acta Psychiatrica Scandinavica,* 1990, *81,* 409–413.

Dixon, L., Krauss, N., Myers, P., and Lehman, A. L. "Clinical and Treatment Correlates of Access to Section 8 Certificates for Homeless Mentally Ill Persons." *Psychiatric Services,* 1994, *45,* 1196–1200.

Drake, R. E., and Noordsy, D. L. "Case Management for People with Coexisting Severe Mental Disorder and Substance Use Disorder." *Psychiatric Annals,* 1994, *24,* 427–431.

Drake, R. E., Osher, F. C., and Wallach, M. A. "Alcohol Use and Abuse in Schizophrenia: A Prospective Community Study." *Journal of Nervous and Mental Disease,* 1989, *177,* 408–414.

Drake, R. E., Osher, F. C., and Wallach, M. A. "Homelessness and Dual Diagnosis." *American Psychologist,* 1991, *46,* 1149–1158.

Drake, R. E., and Wallach, M. A. "Substance Abuse Among the Chronic Mentally Ill." *Hospital and Community Psychiatry,* 1989, *40,* 1041–1046.

Drake, R. E., Wallach, M. A., and Hoffman, J. S. "Housing Instability and Homelessness Among Aftercare Patients of an Urban State Hospital." *Hospital and Community Psychiatry,* 1989, *40,* 46–51.

Drake, R. E., Wallach, M. A., Teague, G. H., Freeman, D. H., Paskus, T. S., and Clark, T. A. "Housing Instability and Homelessness Among Rural Schizophrenic Patients." *American Journal of Psychiatry,* 1991, *148,* 330–336.

Fields, S. "The Relationship Between Residential Treatment and Supported Housing in a Community System of Services." *Psychosocial Rehabilitation Journal,* 1990, *13,* 105–113.

Gaffney, L., and Dixon, L. "Engagement of Homeless Persons in Treatment." Paper presented at the 148th annual meeting of the American Psychiatric Association, Miami, Fla., May 1995. Abstract published in *New Research Program and Abstracts,* 95–96.

Goldfinger, S. M., Schutt, R. K., Seidman, L. M., Turner, W., Penk, W. E., and Tolomiczenko, G. "Alternative Measures of Substance Abuse Among Homeless Mentally Ill Persons in the Cross-Section and Over Time." *Journal of Nervous and Mental Disease,* in press.

Gounis, K., and Susser, E. "Shelterization and Its Implications for Mental Health Services." In N. Cohen (ed.), *Psychiatry Takes to the Streets: Outreach and Crisis Intervention for the Mentally Ill.* New York: Guilford Press, 1990.

Grunberg, J., and Eagle, P. F. "Shelterization: How the Homeless Adapt to Shelter Living." *Hospital and Community Psychiatry,* 1990, *41,* 521–525.

Harp, H. "Independent Living with Support Services: The Goal and Future for Mental Health Consumers." *Psychosocial Rehabilitation Journal,* 1990, *13* (4), 85–89.

Kessler, R. C., McGonagle K. A., Zhao, S., Nelson, C. B., Hughes, M., Eshleman, S., Wittchen, H., and Kendler, K. S. "Lifetime and Twelve-Month Prevalence of DSM-III-R Psychiatric Disorders in the United States." *Archives of General Psychiatry,* 1994, *51,* 8–19.

Kline, J., Harris, M., Bebout, R. E., and Drake, R. E. "Contrasting Integrated and Linkage Models of Treatment for Homeless, Dually Diagnosed Adults." In K. Minkoff and R. E. Drake (eds.), *Dual Diagnosis of Major Mental Illness and Substance Use Disorder.* New Directions for Mental Health Services, no. 50. San Francisco: Jossey-Bass, 1991.

Negrete, J. C., Knapp, W. P., Douglas, D. E., Smith, W. B. "Cannabis Affects the Severity of Schizophrenic Symptoms: Results of a Clinical Survey." *Psychological Medicine,* 1986, *16,* 515–520.

Newman, S. E. "The Severely Mentally Ill Homeless: Housing Needs and Housing Policy." Baltimore, Md.: Johns Hopkins University Institute for Policy Studies, Occasional Paper No. 12, 1992.

Osher, F. C., and Kofoed, L. I. "Treatment of Patients with Psychiatric and Psychoactive Substance Abuse Disorders." *Hospital and Community Psychiatry,* 1989, *40,* 1025–1030.

Osher, F., Drake, R., Noordsy, D., Teague, G. E., Hurlbut, S. C., Biesanz, S. C., and Beaudett, M. S. "Correlates of Outcomes of Alcohol Use Disorder Among Rural Schizophrenic Outpatients." *Journal of Clinical Psychiatry,* 1994, *55,* 109–113.

Petrila, J. "The Supreme Court's Ruling in *Edmonds v. Oxford House:* Implications for Group Homes." *Psychiatric Services,* 1995, *46,* 1011–1012.

Ridgely, M. S., Goldman, H. H., and Willenbring, M. "Barriers to the Care of Persons with Dual Diagnoses: Organizational and Financing Issues." *Schizophrenia Bulletin,* 1990, *16,* 123–132.

Ridgeway, P., and Zipple, A. M. "The Paradigm Shift in Residential Services: From the Linear Continuum to Supported Housing Approaches." *Psychosocial Rehabilitation Journal,* 1990, *13,* 11–31.

Robinson, C. T., Dixon, L., Stewart, B., Harold, J., Lehman, A. F. *Family Connections of the Homeless Mentally Ill.* Poster session, 146th annual meeting of the American Psychiatric Association, San Francisco, Calif., 1993.

Rubinstein, L. *The Impact of the Fair Housing Amendments on Land-Use Regulations Affecting People with Disabilities.* Washington, D.C.: Mental Health Law Project, 1989.

Safer, D. "Substance Abuse by Young Adult Chronic Patients." *Hospital and Community Psychiatry,* 1987, *38,* 511–514.

Schutt, R. K., and Goldfinger, S. M. "Housing Preferences and Perceptions of Health and Functioning Among Homeless Mentally Ill Persons." *Psychiatric Services,* 1996, *47,* 381–386.

Tessler, R. C., and Dennis, D. L. *A Synthesis of NIMH-Funded Research Concerning Persons who Are Homeless and Mentally Ill.* Rockville, Md.: National Institute of Mental Health, 1989.

Ziedonis, D. M., and Fisher, W. "Assessment and Treatment of Comorbid Substance Abuse in Individuals with Schizophrenia." *Psychiatric Annals,* 1994, *24,* 477–483.

*FRED C. OSHER, M.D., is associate professor of psychiatry and director of community psychiatry at the School of Medicine, University of Maryland.*

*LISA B. DIXON, M.D., is associate professor of psychiatry and research psychiatrist at the Center for Mental Health Services, School of Medicine, University of Maryland.*

*Families are critically important sources of housing, financial support, and direct care for persons with dual disorders.*

# Family Support for Persons with Dual Disorders

*Robin E. Clark*

Michael was twenty years old when he was diagnosed with schizophrenia. His family had noticed that he was spending more time alone in his room and that he increasingly voiced thoughts that they found bizarre or frightening. Still, they were surprised when his boss called one day to say that he had begun shouting at co-workers, accusing them of trying to poison him. After three months in a private hospital, a psychiatrist confirmed Michael's diagnosis and prescribed antipsychotic medication. Insurance covered only a portion of the medical bills, so his family took out a second mortgage on their home to pay the additional hospital charges.

In the ensuing years, Michael was rehospitalized a number of times. A local mental health center arranged for him to live in a group home, but he had difficulty complying with the rules and eventually left to live in a rented room downtown. Complaining that it made him feel like "a crash-test dummy" and that he really did not need it, he went for long periods without taking his medication. Michael, who had been a moderate drinker in high school, began getting into minor scrapes with the police when he drank. Sometimes he disappeared for long periods of time. Eventually his family received a call from a distant hospital, police department, or shelter asking them to come take him home.

Relations with his family, which had been tense since his teens, have become even more strained since Michael, now thirty-eight, began to suspect that his parents are conspiring with the FBI to implant "thought amplifiers" in his brain. Fearful of a widening conspiracy, Michael tells his case manager that his family hates him and that he rarely sees them. In spite of their difficulties, Michael's mother continues to call him and often takes him out for lunch and on shopping trips during which she buys him clothes or furnishings for his room. Michael periodically runs out of money toward the end of the month and his parents give him money for food or help him pay his rent. When he gets in trouble with the police or is hospitalized away from home, it is almost always his father who comes to post bail or to take him home.

Michael's father is now in his mid-seventies and is becoming increasingly immobile from arthritis and heart disease. His mother, who spends most of her time looking after Michael and his father, feels isolated and worries about what will happen when she and her husband are no longer able to give Michael the help he needs. Michael worries, too.

## Benefits and Burdens of Family Support

Like Michael, most persons with severe mental illness and substance disorders rely heavily on others to assist them with the basics of daily living. Families are the primary source of much of this help. Recent research suggests that they play a central role in the survival and well-being of their relatives with dual disorders, supplying large amounts of direct care and financial support (Carpentier and others, 1992; Clark and Drake, 1994; Franks, 1990; Tausig, Fisher, and Tessler, 1992). Still, we know relatively little about how families cope with these added demands, how treatment affects clients and families, and how family support—or the lack of it—influences a person's recovery from mental illness and substance disorders. As a consequence of our lack of understanding, treatment providers often underestimate the importance of families in the lives of their clients with dual disorders.

Persons with severe mental illness who also abuse alcohol or other drugs have difficulty managing tasks of daily living and have higher rates of unemployment than do persons with mental illness alone (Drake and Wallach, 1989; Kay, Kalathara, and Meinzer, 1989). Because of these problems they often depend on families or friends for assistance in securing the basic necessities of life. Although families make many other important contributions to their relatives, the basic assistance they give is, for many persons with dual disorders, a primary means of survival and the foundation on which formal treatment and rehabilitative services are built. Without first satisfying these primary needs, persons with dual disorders are unlikely to participate in or respond fully to treatment interventions.

Having a relative with dual disorders clearly places significant additional demands on families. A study of New Hampshire parents with adult children revealed that when a son or daughter had a dual disorder they spent over twice as much time giving direct care and contributed significantly more financial support than when their children were free of chronic illnesses (Clark, 1994). Parents of persons with dual disorders spent a good deal more time providing general care, for example, cooking and cleaning. They also spent more time giving rides, intervening in crises, and creating structured leisure activities for their relatives. A comparable amount of service provided by formal caregivers—case managers or home health aides, for example—would have cost almost $14,000 per year in 1992 dollars. Economic support given by parents in the dual disorder group totaled almost 16 percent of their annual income, whereas comparison families contributed an amount equal to about 6 percent of their annual income.

Family support may also have different long-term results for recipients. Financial assistance for adult children without dual disorders tends to be for purposes that could be considered investments, such as college tuition or a downpayment on a car or house. Economic support for persons with dual disorders is most often for basic necessities like food, clothing, or shelter. For persons without dual disorders, family assistance may provide a boost to economic status or earning potential. For those with dual disorders, family assistance has the far more immediate consequence of ensuring adequate nutrition and a place to stay. Losing this support could have serious consequences.

Homelessness is a potential result of lost family support. Although being homeless is stressful in itself, it also increases the risk that one will acquire AIDS, or be assaulted, robbed, or incarcerated (Fisher and Breakey, 1991; Torres, Mani, Altholz, and Brickner, 1990). Evidence for a connection between lack of family support and homelessness comes from separate studies of men and women with schizophrenia in the New York area conducted by Caton and others (1994, 1995). Matching one hundred men with schizophrenia currently living in a homeless shelter with one hundred who were similar in other characteristics but who had never been homeless, Caton and her colleagues found that a lack of adequate current family support was more strongly associated with homelessness than any of the other variables they considered. Positive psychiatric symptoms, drug abuse, antisocial personality, and treatment engagement were also important in explaining differences between the two groups, but less so than current family assistance in the form of money, shelter, food, clothing, advice, and companionship. A second study of homeless women produced very similar results: inadequate current family support was again the factor most strongly associated with homelessness (Caton and others, 1995).

In a separate study Tessler and others (1992) found that persons with mental illness who had been homeless during the previous year were more dissatisfied with and had less faith in their families than those who had not been homeless. Families of the homeless group reported less involvement, gave less care, and had more negative attitudes toward them than families of the never-homeless group. When combined with other patient characteristics such as gender, deficits in daily living, work, and incarceration history, however, family variables were not significantly associated with previous homelessness.

Although family support may benefit persons with dual disorders it can also be a burden to families. Intuitively it seems likely that substance abuse would add to the burden that families of persons with severe mental illness feel, but current research does not allow us to confirm or refute this supposition or to say how much more burden substance abuse might add.

Typically family burden is seen as a combination of objective (how much families do) and subjective (how they feel about what they do) factors (Hoenig and Hamilton, 1966; Thompson and Doll, 1982). Family caregivers may perform certain types of tasks frequently, such as preparing meals, but may not feel especially burdened by them. Other tasks, like restraining an intoxicated or angry relative, occur less often but are experienced as more burdensome.

Tessler and Gamache (1994) have further refined tasks assisted by families according to whether they are related to care (routine support) or control (behavioral problems). Care items mentioned frequently include providing transportation, time and money management, and preparing meals. Control items include attention seeking, night disturbances, embarrassing behavior, substance abuse, and a range of other troublesome behaviors (Tessler and Gamache, 1994). Some studies indicate that family members experience the care tasks as more burdensome; this finding may be influenced, however, by specific characteristics of the groups studied or by the relative infrequency of control tasks (Maurin and Boyd, 1990). Logically one would expect that persons with dual disorders would require more family efforts to control behaviors than persons with mental illness alone. It is less clear how dual disorders might affect the amount of general supportive care required.

## Factors That Influence Family Support

The sheer burden of caring for a relative with multiple problems might seem enough to discourage families, but the New York study of homeless men did not find differences in the level of burden reported by families of homeless and domiciled men (Caton and others, 1994). The two groups did score differently on an index of family disorganization. Men in the homeless group were over four times more likely to come from families that were inconsistent in nurturing, had unstable housing, inadequate income, and relied on public assistance. Parents of men in this group were more likely to have a history of criminal involvement, mental illness, and substance abuse. Family history does not appear to be strongly associated with homelessness among women with schizophrenia (Caton and others, 1995).

It is not entirely clear from this study why traditional patterns of family support break down. Low family support could be the result rather than the cause of homelessness, but the combination of differences between the two groups in reported family histories of disorganization and similarities in levels of current family burden suggests that the seeds of lower support are sown before the men become homeless. Families beset by extreme poverty, illness, and a range of other problems are likely to have fewer resources to give to their relatives than do others. It is important to note that not all of the study subjects came from impoverished, disorganized families, and that current behaviors like psychiatric symptoms and substance abuse are also associated with homelessness.

Although poor family support and substance abuse are both associated with homelessness, this does not necessarily mean that families of persons with dual disorders are unwilling or unable to help. Most give substantial amounts of economic and direct care support to their relatives despite active substance use. As substance abuse becomes more severe, the amount of economic support that families give decreases, but the amount of direct care appears to be unaffected (Clark and Drake, 1994).

When it comes to living together, drug and alcohol use seem to exert a more complex influence on family decisions. In an unpublished statewide survey of over 2,000 people receiving publicly funded treatment for severe mental illness in New Hampshire, clients who used alcohol were significantly less likely to live with their families. This could be interpreted as evidence that families are less willing to house a substance-abusing relative. However, there are other explanations for the finding. For example, people who do not live with their families may have less supervision and are therefore more likely to abuse drugs or alcohol; substance abusers initially may be more socially competent and therefore may be more likely to form relationships outside the home; different living situations may reflect different levels of psychiatric impairment that may be related in turn to substance abuse.

Another study of persons enrolled in specialized treatment for dual disorders suggests that parents are more willing than other relatives to house someone who is actively abusing substances (Clark and Drake, 1994). Persons who abuse drugs or alcohol more severely are less likely to live with relatives in general. When they do live with family, they are more likely to live with parents than with siblings or other relatives. This somewhat confusing picture may be explained by thinking of parents as service or housing providers of last resort.

Substance abuse decreases the range of available living options. The New Hampshire study indicates that substance abuse is associated with more stress and less appropriate housing wherever the person lives. This is generally consistent with other data that show that persons with dual disorders tend to live in less desirable housing (Uehara, 1994). When their adult children with dual disorders leave or are asked to leave their present accommodations, parents may, with some reluctance, be their only housing option. In one survey of family caregivers for persons with schizophrenia, over two-thirds of whom were parents, practical concerns like "being able to keep an eye on the patient's drinking" were the benefits of living together that caregivers cited most frequently (Winefield and Harvey, 1994). Filial relationships seem to be a critical buffer against homelessness for persons with dual disorders.

Housing a relative with dual disorders is not purely a burden; relatives with mental illness often contribute positively to their families, both financially and otherwise (Greenberg, Greenley, and Benedict, 1994). Still, living together is not without its risks. Increased contact is associated with more family stress, particularly for spouses and parents (Anderson and Lynch, 1984; Winefield and Harvey, 1994). Living together increases the risk that parents or spouses will be assaulted (Gondolf, Mulvey, and Lidz, 1990; Straznickas, McNiel, and

Binder, 1993). Substance abuse seems to increase further the likelihood that the relative with mental illness will threaten or attack a family member (Monahan, 1992; Swan and Lavitt, 1988). Families who house a relative with a dual disorder are thus particularly in need of support.

Cohabitation may also be difficult for the person with a dual disorder. About one-fourth of persons with severe mental illness say they prefer to live with their families (Massey and Wu, 1993). It is not clear if substance abuse alters these preferences. In most cases persons with mental illness and their families agree on the decision to live together, but substance abuse may reduce consensus. Disagreement about the desirability of living together leads to conflict and dissatisfaction. Stressful family atmospheres are associated with increased relapse rates (Kashner and others, 1991; Kavanagh, 1992), and persons with dual disorders report more dissatisfaction with family relations and a greater desire for family treatment than do persons with mental illness alone (Dixon, McNary, and Lehman, 1995). Moreover, evidence linking parental substance abuse to current substance abuse by adult offspring means that in some cases the family environment may not be conducive to controlling substance abuse (Gershon and others, 1988; Noordsy, Drake, Biesanz, and McHugo, 1994).

Even though increased contact, behavioral problems, and greater demands for direct care add to family burden, there is no clear relationship between these stressors and a family's decision to terminate support for a relative with dual disorders. Evidence from studies of family caregivers for elderly relatives who are frail or have Alzheimer's disease suggests that the decision is influenced by a combination of the ill relative's behavior, the family's financial resources, and their attitudes toward caregiving. One study found that family caregivers were more likely to place their relatives with Alzheimer's disease in a nursing home when they felt frustrated or trapped by the caregiving role (Aneshensel, Pearlin, and Schuler, 1993). Other factors such as more severe functional impairment, caregiver stress, and having enough money to pay for out-of-home care were also associated, albeit more weakly, with the decision to place.

Help and emotional support from other family members almost certainly make the difficult aspects of caregiving more bearable. Single caregivers report more stress than married ones (Carpentier and others, 1992). Family cohesiveness and support appear to be particularly important in reducing the frustration that family caregivers feel (Greenberg, Seltzer, and Greenley, 1993). The extent to which burden can be reduced or to which family ties can be maintained by formal services is still unknown.

Many families continue providing direct and financial support in the face of great demands and stress. Why some families continue and others distance themselves from their relatives with dual disorders is a puzzle whose answer has important implications for relatives, treatment providers, and families. Preserving family support has obvious benefits for persons with dual disorders and probably for their families as well. Knowing what factors lead to family estrangement would enable more appropriately focused interventions to prevent family breakup.

## Treatment and Family Relationships

Because there are few longitudinal studies of family support, we know almost nothing about how treatment of persons with dual disorders affects family support or what roles families play in recovery. Evidence from the mental health literature provides some clues. For example, it seems logical to conclude that treatment that reduces hospitalization will increase family contact and will thereby lead to greater family burden (see, for example, Goldman, 1982), but there is little recent documentation to support this notion. Most studies find no relationship between amount of hospitalization and measures of objective or subjective family burden (Maurin and Boyd, 1990). One study reported that families of persons who received intensive community services and less hospital care than customary actually preferred the community intervention (Reynolds and Hoult, 1984).

There appears to be little difference in the impact of various client-focused treatments on families, but interventions that target families (primarily families of persons with schizophrenia) have specifically shown significant changes in patterns of family interaction and in patient relapse rates (Bellack and Mueser, 1993).

Two studies illustrate these findings. Falloon and others (1982) compared in-home family therapy to individual treatment for a small group of patients with schizophrenia who were receiving psychotropic medication. Over a nine-month period, patients in the family therapy group had significantly fewer relapses and lower levels of psychiatric symptoms than those who participated only in individual treatment. In a larger study, Hogarty and others (1986) compared the effects of a family-focused intervention to those of individual treatment for patients with schizophrenia who came from high *expressed emotion* households. Expressed emotion covers a range of strong negative affects in family interactions, particularly criticism and emotional overinvolvement. After one year of treatment, patients whose families participated in a psychoeducational intervention designed to "lower the emotional climate of the home while maintaining reasonable expectations for patient performance" had significantly fewer relapses than persons whose families did not participate. No patients relapsed in families who successfully changed from high to low expressed emotion status. Although neither of the studies discussed above focused specifically on persons with dual disorders, the high levels of dissatisfaction with family relations among persons with dual disorders suggest that family-focused interventions may prove beneficial for them as well.

Interventions that attempt to improve family interactions have sometimes been criticized for focusing only on the family's response to the identified relative's behavior rather than on the behavior of both parties (Kanter, Lamb, and Loeper, 1987). Evidence suggests that the combination of difficult behaviors presented by the person with mental illness and his or her family's reactions contribute to the phenomenon known as expressed emotion (Kavanagh, 1992). Approaches that blame either party for relationship difficulties are likely to be less effective than those that view expressed emotion as an interactive phenomenon. Although recent theories posit a more complex interaction between persons with mental illness and their families (Maurin and Boyd, 1990; Mueser and Glynn, 1990), it is not clear that those ideas have been widely incorporated into treatment practice.

We do not know whether there is any association between the criticism and emotional overinvolvement that characterize high expressed emotion situations and the amounts of direct caregiving and economic assistance that families provide. This is an area in which further research may help. For now we should be careful not to confuse the amount of objective family support with the emotional content of family interactions. We cannot assume that emotional overinvolvement means that the family is giving too much direct support or that families who are giving a great deal of support are doing so inappropriately.

A limitation of virtually all treatment studies that include measures of family burden is that they tend to be relatively brief, often lasting for a year or less. Recent work by Tessler and Gamache (1994) suggests that continuity of service rather than the type or intensity of treatment a person receives may be a critical factor in reducing the burden that person's family experiences. In their analysis of data from three sites in Ohio, Tessler and Gamache found a significant relationship between the continuity of a relative's treatment and aspects of family burden for families with whom the client lived. They defined continuity as having a case manager or other formal caregiver who "helped them plan and obtain the services they needed" at each of three points over a two-year period. Continuity did not have the same benefits for families who lived separately from study participants. Consistent with other studies, being a parent and sharing a residence were associated with higher levels of family burden.

Family services specifically designed for persons with dual disorders, a relatively new phenomenon, are often incorporated into integrated treatment programs (Fox, Fox, and Drake, 1992; Sciacca, 1991). Most take a group psychoeducational approach that provides information about the effects of substance use for persons with mental illness and discusses strategies for behavior management (Clark and Drake, 1992). Typical psychoeducational groups are shorter in duration than the groups for families of persons with schizophrenia mentioned earlier; information on substance abuse can easily be incorporated into long-term family groups, however (Ryglewicz, 1991).

As yet there is little information about the effectiveness of family interventions specifically targeted for relatives of persons with dual disorders. Additional research could help determine the effectiveness of these approaches for persons with psychiatric diagnoses other than schizophrenia. Existing research and clinical opinion suggest that a "one size fits all" approach may not be appropriate for family services (Pfeiffer and Mostek, 1991). Not only may different psychiatric diagnoses present different problems, but family members may experience them differently depending on their relationship to the person with a dual disorder. Spouses, who often drop out of family groups composed primarily of parents, are more likely to remain engaged in a group of their peers (Mannion, Mueser, and Solomon, 1994). Evidence also shows that siblings have views of their brothers and sisters with mental illness that are substantially different from those of their parents (Horwitz, Tessler, Fisher, and Gamache, 1992). Services must be tailored to fit differing needs of family members.

One area of potential conflict between persons with dual disorders and their families is money management. Persons with dual disorders may have a particularly difficult time managing their funds (Drake and Wallach, 1989). Families often become involved as informal money managers or more formally as payees for government programs like supplemental security income or social security disability insurance. Although money management is a frequent subject of disagreement within families, it can be an effective way of reducing substance abuse and relapse rates (Spittle, 1991). Whether or not families are the most appropriate money managers is currently debated, but the fact is that many family members find themselves in that role. Given its potential importance, this issue should be addressed explicitly in psychoeducational interventions for families.

Although research shows that substance abuse has negative consequences for families as well as for persons with dual disorders, families often do not make the connection between substance abuse and these difficulties. In one survey of preferences for additional education, families whose relatives had schizophrenia ranked information on drug and alcohol abuse last on a list of forty-five topics; families whose relatives had a major affective disorder ranked the topic slightly higher at thirty-second out of forty-five (Mueser and others, 1992). Other studies show that families often do not see incidents of drug or alcohol abuse as particularly disturbing (Gubman, Tessler, and Willis, 1987; Hatfield, 1978). In contrast, families usually do report behaviors that are associated with substance abuse—such as temper tantrums, violence, or symptom exacerbations—as disturbing or stressful. Thus families' apparent lack of interest in substance abuse problems could stem from their attribution of behavioral problems to the mental disorder rather than to substance abuse.

Just as persons with dual disorders go through progressive phases of treatment readiness, from engagement to persuasion to active treatment (Drake and others, 1993), families may also need to be convinced that the formal treatment system has something helpful to offer them. Many families feel frustrated or disappointed about their relationships with the providers who serve their relatives and may be wary of offers to help (Hanson and Rapp, 1992). An unknown percentage of families have little or no contact with their relatives and therefore may be particularly difficult to engage (Wasow, 1994). A cooperative approach to working with families, one that recognizes and appreciates their knowledge and skills, is needed to establish a trusting, working relationship with families. This does not mean that treatment providers should wait for families to make the first move. An assertive but respectful approach to establishing a relationship with families is likely to be most effective.

## Clinical Implications of Family Support

The goals of provider-family relationships are multifaceted. Providers may be able to reduce some of the stress or burden on families by providing timely crisis response and training in management of substance abuse and other behavioral problems. As emphasized in earlier schizophrenia studies, support and education for families can benefit clients by reducing relapse rates and perhaps improving symptoms. Providers can also learn a great deal from families that will help them anticipate crises and generally improve treatment effectiveness. Better provider-family relationships are likely to benefit all parties.

Maintaining family ties is a critically important goal of treatment and rehabilitation that has largely been ignored. Recent research documents the potential life-saving benefits of the basic support that families give. Although the strains that dual disorders place on family relations can cause providers, families, or their relatives with dual disorders to conclude that a respite is needed, the value of maintaining strong family ties should not be discounted.

Informal discussions with treatment providers suggest that they are often unaware of the substantial amounts of direct care and economic support that families give their clients. The reasons for this are not clear. Perhaps their clients prefer to keep such matters private, or perhaps providers do not ask about family support. In either case, the result is that providers may not fully appreciate the vital role that families play in the lives of their clients. Studies indicate that although the amount of family support varies widely, the percentage of families who give direct or financial support is impressive (Clark, 1994; Franks, 1990). Current clinical assessment techniques focus on problems in family relations but are not adequate for documenting family support. Providers may need to make a special effort to understand the extent to which a family gives concrete support to a client. This often means talking directly with the family about the kinds of support they extend in a typical month (see Clark, 1994 or Clark and Drake, 1994 for examples of support categories).

Although the intensity of conflict may lead providers and family members to conclude that a temporary separation is necessary, the potential negative impact of emotional conflict should be weighed against possible loss of family support that can be caused by separation. Indeed, preservation and enhancement of family support systems should be considered an important measure of treatment effectiveness.

## Conclusion

Despite the stresses imposed by severe mental illness and substance abuse, families play a critical role in the lives of most persons with dual disorders. That role is broader than the one traditionally afforded them by treatment providers. Family concerns include not only their effect on clinical outcomes and the inevitable difficulties they encounter in caring for a relative with a severe, chronic illness, but also the effects of the direct support they give in the form of time, money, and in-kind gifts.

Although community mental health and psychosocial rehabilitation programs place a high premium on helping persons with severe mental illness to live independently, independence cannot be achieved at the expense of informal social support from family and friends. Improved functioning may reduce reliance on these systems, but evidence from surveys of the general population shows that mutual support among family members throughout the lifespan is overwhelmingly the norm rather than the exception (MacDonald, 1989; Marks, 1993). Perhaps a more fitting goal than independence, one that reflects more accurately the experience of most people, is *effective interdependence*. Such a goal suggests that optimal functioning, or, to use a term from psychosocial rehabilitation, recovery, is not something a person achieves independently but rather in the context of a supportive system. Research suggests that this system is particularly important for the survival of persons with dual disorders. This view has yet to be fully integrated into current treatment interventions for persons with dual disorders. Incorporating services that strengthen family relationships is a challenge that clinicians and policy makers must learn to meet.

## References

Anderson, E. A., and Lynch, M. M. "A Family Impact Analysis: The Deinstitutionalization of the Mentally Ill." *Family Relations,* 1984, *33,* 41–46.

Aneshensel, C. S., Pearlin, L. I., and Schuler, R. H. "Stress, Role Captivity, and the Cessation of Caregiving." *Journal of Health and Social Behavior,* 1993, *34,* 54–70.

Bellack, A. S., and Mueser, K. T. "Psychosocial Treatment for Schizophrenia." *Schizophrenia Bulletin,* 1993, *19,* 317–336.

Carpentier, N., Lesage, A., Goulet, J., Lalonde, P., and Renaud, M. "Burden of Care of Families Not Living with Young Schizophrenic Relatives." *Hospital and Community Psychiatry,* 1992, *43* (1), 38–43.

Caton, C.L.M., Shrout, P. E., Dominguez, B., Eagle, P. F., Opler, L. A., and Cournos, F. "Risk Factors for Homelessness Among Women with Schizophrenia." *American Journal of Public Health,* 1995, *85* (8), 1153–1156.

Caton, C.L.M., Shrout, P. E., Eagle, P. F., Opler, L. A., Felix, A., and Dominguez, B. "Risk Factors for Homelessness Among Schizophrenic Men: A Case-Control Study." *American Journal of Public Health,,* 1994, *84* (2), 265–270.

Clark, R. E. "Family Costs Associated with Severe Mental Illness and Substance Use." *Hospital and Community Psychiatry,* 1994, *45* (8), 808–813.

Clark, R. E., and Drake, R. E. "Substance Abuse and Mental Illness: What Families Need to Know." *Innovations and Research,* 1992, *1* (4), 3–8.

Clark, R. E., and Drake, R. E. "Expenditures of Time and Money by Families of People with Severe Mental Illness and Substance Use Disorders." *Community Mental Health Journal,* 1994, *30* (2), 145–163.

Dixon, L., McNary, S., and Lehman, A. "Substance Abuse and Family Relationships of Persons with Severe Mental Illness." *American Journal of Psychiatry,* 1995, *152* (3), 456–458.

Drake, R. E., Bartels, S. J., Teague, G. B., Noordsy, D. L., and Clark, R. E. "Treatment of Substance Abuse in Severely Mentally Ill Patients." *Journal of Nervous and Mental Disease,* 1993, *181* (10), 606–610.

Drake, R. E., and Wallach, M. A. "Substance Abuse Among the Chronic Mentally Ill." *Hospital and Community Psychiatry,* 1989, *40* (10), 1041–1046.

Falloon, I.R.H., Boyd, J. L., McGill, C. W., Razani, J., Moss, H. B., and Gilderman, A. M. "Family Management in the Prevention of Exacerbations of Schizophrenia: A Controlled Study." *New England Journal of Medicine,* 1982, *306* (24), 1437–1440.

Fisher, P. J., and Breakey, W. R. "The Epidemiology of Alcohol, Drug, and Mental Disorders Among Homeless Persons." *American Psychologist,* 1991, *46* (11), 1115–1128.

Fox, T., Fox, L., and Drake, R. E. "Developing a Statewide Service System for People with Co-Occurring Mental Illness and Substance Use Disorders." *Innovations and Research,* 1992, *1* (4), 9–14.

Franks, D. D. "Economic Contribution of Families Caring for Persons with Severe and Persistent Mental Illness." *Administration and Policy in Mental Health,* 1990, *18* (1), 9–18.

Gershon, E. S., Delisi, L. E., Hamovit, J., Nurnberger, J. I., Maxwell, M. E., Schreiber, J., Dauphinais, D., Dingman, C. W., and Guroff, J. J. "A Controlled Family Study of Chronic Psychoses: Schizophrenia and Schizoaffective Disorder." *Archives of General Psychiatry,* 1988, *45,* 328–336.

Goldman, H. H. "Mental Illness and Family Burden: A Public Health Perspective." *Hospital and Community Psychiatry,* 1982, *33* (7), 557–560.

Gondolf, E. W., Mulvey, E. P., and Lidz, G. W. "Characteristics of Perpetrators of Family and Nonfamily Assaults." *Hospital and Community Psychiatry,* 1990, *41* (2), 191–193.

Greenberg, J. S., Greenley, J. R., and Benedict, P. "Contributions of Persons with Serious Mental Illness to Their Families." *Hospital and Community Psychiatry,* 1994, *45* (5), 475–480.

Greenberg, J. S., Seltzer, M. M., and Greenley, J. R. "Aging Parents of Adults with Disabilities: The Gratifications and Frustrations of Later-Life Caregiving." *Gerontologist,* 1993, *33* (4), 542–550.

Gubman, G. D., Tessler, R. C., and Willis, G. "Living with the Mentally Ill: Factors Affecting Household Complaints." *Schizophrenia Bulletin,* 1987, *13* (4), 727–736.

Hanson, J. G., and Rapp, C. A. "Families' Perceptions of Community Mental Health Programs for Their Relatives with a Severe Mental Illness." *Community Mental Health Journal,* 1992, *28* (3), 181–197.

Hatfield, A. B. "Psychological Costs of Schizophrenia to the Family." *Social Work,* 1978, *23,* 355–359.

Hoenig, J., and Hamilton, M. W. "The Schizophrenic Patient in the Community and His Effect on the Household." *International Journal of Social Psychiatry,* 1966, *12* (3), 165–176.

Hogarty, G. E., Anderson, C. M., Reiss, D. J., Kornblith, S. J., Greenwald, D. P., Javna, C. D., and Madonia, M. J. "Family Psychoeducation, Social Skills Training, and Maintenance Chemotherapy in the Aftercare Treatment of Schizophrenia." *Archives of General Psychiatry,* 1986, *43,* 633–642.

Horwitz, A., Tessler, R., Fisher, G., and Gamache, G. "The Role of Adult Siblings in Providing Social Support to the Seriously Mentally Ill." *Journal of Marriage and the Family,* 1992, *54,* 233–241.

Kanter, J., Lamb, H. R., and Loeper, C. "Expressed Emotion in Families: A Critical Review." *Hospital and Community Psychiatry,* 1987, *38* (4), 374–380.

Kashner, T. M., Rader, L. E., Rodell, D. E., Beck, C. M., Rodell, L. R., and Muller, K. "Family Characteristics, Substance Abuse, and Hospitalization Patterns of Patients with Schizophrenia." *Hospital and Community Psychiatry,* 1991, *42* (2), 195–197.

Kavanagh, D. J. "Recent Developments in Expressed Emotion and Schizophrenia." *British Journal of Psychiatry,* 1992, *160,* 601–620.

Kay, S. R., Kalathara, M., and Meinzer, A. E. "Diagnostic and Behavioral Characteristics of Psychiatric Patients Who Abuse Substances." *Hospital and Community Psychiatry*, 1989, *40* (10), 1061–1064.

MacDonald, M. M. *Family Background, the Life Cycle, and Inter-Household Transfers*. National Survey of Families and Households working paper no. 13. Madison, Wis., Center for Demography and Ecology, University of Wisconsin, Madison, 1989.

Mannion, E., Mueser, K., and Solomon, P. "Designing Psychoeducational Services for Spouses of Persons with Serious Mental Illness." *Community Mental Health Journal*, 1994, *30* (2), 177–190.

Marks, N. F. *Caregiving Across the Life-Span: A New National Profile*. National Survey of Families and Households working paper no. 55. Madison, Wis., Center for Demography and Ecology, University of Wisconsin, Madison, 1993.

Massey, O. T., and Wu, L. "Service Delivery and Community Housing: Perspectives of Consumers, Family Members, and Case Managers." *Innovations and Research*, 1993, *2* (3), 9–15.

Maurin, J. T., and Boyd, C. B. "Burden of Mental Illness on the Family: A Critical Review." *Archives of Psychiatric Nursing*, 1990, *4* (2), 99–107.

Monahan, J. "Mental Disorder and Violent Behavior: Perceptions and Evidence." *American Psychologist*, 1992, *47* (4), 511–521.

Mueser, K. T., and Glynn, S. M. "Behavioral Family Therapy for Schizophrenia." In M. Hersen, R. M. Eisler, and P. M. Miller (eds.), *Progress in Behavior Modification*. Vol. 16. Newbury Park, Calif.: Sage, 1990.

Mueser, K. T., Bellack, A. S., Wade, J. H., Sayers, S. L., and Rosenthal, C. K. "An Assessment of the Educational Needs of Chronic Psychiatric Patients and Their Relatives." *British Journal of Psychiatry*, 1992, *160*, 674–680.

Noordsy, D. L., Drake, R. E., Biesanz, J. C., and McHugo, G. J. "Family History of Alcoholism in Schizophrenia." *Journal of Nervous and Mental Disease*, 1994, *182* (11), 651–655.

Pfeiffer, E. J., and Mostek, M. "Services for Families of People with Mental Illness." *Hospital and Community Psychiatry*, 1991, *42* (3), 262–264.

Reynolds, I., and Hoult, J. E. "The Relatives of the Mentally Ill: A Comparative Trial of Community-Oriented and Hospital-Oriented Psychiatric Care." *Journal of Nervous and Mental Disease*, 1984, *172* (8), 480–489.

Ryglewicz, H. "Psychoeducation for Clients and Families: A Way In, Out, and Through in Working with People with Dual Disorders." *Psychosocial Rehabilitation Journal*, 1991, *15* (2), 79–89.

Sciacca, K. "An Integrated Treatment Approach for Severely Mentally Ill Individuals with Substance Disorders." In K. Minkoff and R. Drake (eds.), *Dual Diagnosis of Major Mental Illness and Substance Disorder*. New Directions for Mental Health Services, no. 50. San Francisco: Jossey-Bass, 1991.

Spittle, B. "The Effect of Financial Management on Alcohol-Related Hospitalization." *American Journal of Psychiatry*, 1991, *148* (2), 221–223.

Straznickas, K. A., McNiel, D. E., and Binder, R. L. "Violence Toward Family Caregivers by Mentally Ill Relatives." *Hospital and Community Psychiatry*, 1993, *44* (4), 385–387.

Swan, R. W., and Lavitt, M. "Patterns of Adjustment to Violence in Families of the Mentally Ill." *Journal of Interpersonal Violence*, 1988, *3* (1), 42–54.

Tausig, M., Fisher, G. A., and Tessler, R. C. "Informal Systems of Care for the Chronically Mentally Ill." *Community Mental Health Journal*, 1992, *28* (5), 413–425.

Tessler, R., and Gamache, G. "Continuity of Care, Residence, and Family Burden in Ohio." *Milbank Quarterly*, 1994, *72* (1), 149–169.

Tessler, R. C., Gamache, G. M., Rossi, P. H., Lehman, A. F., and Goldman, H. H. "The Kindred Bonds of Mentally Ill Homeless Persons." *New England Journal of Public Policy*, 1992, *8* (1), 265–280.

Thompson, E. H., Jr., and Doll, W. "The Burden of Families Coping with the Mentally Ill: An Invisible Crisis." *Family Relations*, 1982, *31*, 379–388.

Torres, R. A., Mani, S., Altholz, J., and Brickner, P. W. "Human Immunodeficiency Virus Infection Among Homeless Men in a New York City Shelter." *Archives of Internal Medicine,* 1990, *150* (10), 2030–2036.

Uehara, E. S. "Race, Gender, and Housing Inequality: An Exploration of the Correlates of Low-Quality Housing Among Clients Diagnosed with Severe and Persistent Mental Illness." *Journal of Health and Social Behavior,* 1994, *35,* 309–321.

Wasow, M. "A Missing Group in Family Research: Parents Not in Contact with Their Mentally Ill Children." *Hospital and Community Psychiatry,* 1994, *45* (7), 720–721.

Winefield, H. R., and Harvey, E. J. "Needs of Family Caregivers in Chronic Schizophrenia." *Schizophrenia Bulletin,* 1994, *20* (3), 557–566.

*ROBIN E. CLARK, Ph.D., is assistant professor of community and family medicine and psychiatry at the Dartmouth Medical School, research associate at the New Hampshire–Dartmouth Psychiatric Research Center, and director of the cost-effectiveness laboratory at Dartmouth Medical School.*

*Across several indicators of psychosocial adjustment, psychiatric and substance abuse symptoms, and mental health service costs, standard mental health care augmented by the behavioral skills intervention model was more effective in improving client outcomes and reducing total service costs for those with dual disorders than case management or modified twelve-step recovery.*

# Cost-Effective Treatment for Persons with Dual Disorders

*Jeanette M. Jerrell*

Concurrent mental and substance disorders are highly prevalent in both the treated mental health (over 50 percent) and general populations (about 16 percent) (Kessler and others, 1994), and are clinically challenging. Persons with co-occurring serious mental illness and substance disorders are difficult to treat and the course of their psychiatric treatment is worsened by substance abuse (Chen and others, 1992). The combination of alcohol and other drug abuse and severe mental illness has been found to be associated with more severe psychiatric symptomatology (Barbee and others, 1989), higher rates of relapse and rehospitalization (Bassuk, 1980), less history of drug or alcohol treatment, more admissions to emergency rooms, noncompliance with pharmacological and psychosocial interventions (Solomon, 1986; Lyons and McGovern, 1989), and increased suicidal and criminal behavior (Safer, 1987; Caton, 1981; Richardson, Craig, and Haughland, 1985). Clinical care providers must deal with these dual problems more effectively to stabilize clients, improve their functioning, and control costs.

From a clinical perspective the question of greatest concern is, "What intervention approaches are effective in dealing with the functional impairment and symptomatology related to dual disorders?" For a clinical manager, there is an equally important second question: "How can overall mental health service costs be contained while providing effective service?" Approaches that show promise for more effectively serving dually diagnosed clients exist in both

This work was supported by a grant from the National Institute of Mental Health (R01-MH46331). The opinions expressed herein do not necessarily represent those of the funding agency. The author thanks Kristin Wieduwilt for performing the data analyses.

the substance abuse and mental health treatment literature and practice, but most have not been systematically tested with individuals who have dual disorders. A few studies, such as that by Bartels and others (1993), describe the differences in service utilization and costs among clients diagnosed as schizophrenic with and without co-occurring substance abuse, but no other studies examining both the costs and effects of substance abuse interventions for the severely mentally ill are reported in the literature.

In this chapter, pertinent results from a controlled cost-effectiveness study comparing three substance abuse intervention approaches for treating persons with co-occurring severe mental illness and substance abuse are summarized. The implications of these findings for clinical managers and care providers to persons with dual disorders are then discussed. The purpose of this presentation is to illustrate the importance of comparing both cost and effectiveness data in assessing alternative intervention strategies. The goal of a cost-effectiveness analysis is to assess which treatment gets better results for the least expense. It is also important to estimate the more general direct service costs associated with caring for a patient (for example, hospitalization or long-term care) or the societal costs of maintaining the patient in the community (for example, medical, social service, or family costs); however, this presentation focuses exclusively on the mental health service costs involved in caring for dual-diagnosis clients, since these costs typically represent the vast majority of public funding for these clients (usually 80 percent to 90 percent of their total care) and are most directly under the control of clinicians and clinical managers.

The analyses presented here focus on describing the mental health cost differences in serving clients across the three interventions and on relating these costs to the functional changes accrued from participation in the three intervention approaches. Although front-line clinicians typically are more interested in the personal benefits to clients than in the supportive costs involved in achieving these changes, the results of changes in client use of intensive mental health services—that is, inpatient, emergency, skilled nursing, and residential treatment facility days—will be meaningful to clinicians as another indicator of stability and enhanced functioning in the community. On the other hand, clinical managers must be concerned with the various program resources needed by clinicians to achieve changes in client problems or functioning.

## Study Setting

The study was conducted in a large, urban setting within a public mental health authority that served about 5,500 severely mentally ill clients over a one-year period. About half of these clients were thought to have some level of co-occurring substance abuse and mental illness; clinicians, clinical managers, families, and frequently the clients themselves were concerned that mental health care and community stability were undermined by problems associated with substance disorders. Some of these clients were repeatedly being served in the acute and subacute components of the service system, whereas others were homeless or involved in the criminal justice system. None was receiving the types of services needed to stabilize them in the community or to attain a reasonable quality of life. Joint training and case consultations were instituted between mental health and drug and alcohol staff prior to the start of this study, and more dual-diagnosis treatment groups were held, some of which were jointly led by staff from both departments. None of these efforts, however, was found to address the magnitude of the problem over the long term. In this context, then, this services research study involving three intervention models at five mental health centers was initiated. The research study was designed to answer questions about which intervention strategy would be most effective in augmenting the usual mental health care for the large, heterogeneous group of severely mentally ill clients with co-occurring substance abuse who were difficult to treat in traditional outpatient mental health clinics.

## Program Implementation

From the various therapeutic approaches that showed promise for use with the dually diagnosed target group, three were chosen for comparative examination in this study. Although there was some variability in the implementation of these program models across mental health centers, the three interventions aimed at the co-occurring substance disorders can be described as follows: In the *twelve-step recovery model*, clinical staff (some in personal recovery) offered transitional groups or mock Alcoholics Anonymous (AA) meetings within the mental health center, took or referred clients to community AA meetings, attempted to facilitate the development of a sponsor relationship for the client, and provided ongoing supportive counseling to help the client manage the twelve-step recovery process. The *behavioral skills training model* relied extensively on a psychoeducational approach for teaching clients self-management skills and then engaging them in repeated practice and reinforcement of these skills. The skills were taught in group sessions that met once a week and the groups were conducted by two licensed clinicians. Social and Independent Living Skills (SILS) modules (Eckman, Liberman, Phipps, and Blair, 1990; Liberman, Massel, Mosk, and Wong, 1985) were covered as well as relapse prevention skills. The *case management model* involved fairly intensive assistance by a clinician or paraprofessional in such areas as housing, daily living skills, legal problems, money management, personal relationships, and leisure time activities. The problems addressed by these interventions included inadequate skills in activities of daily living, low stress tolerance, poor impulse control, use and abuse of alcohol and street drugs, dependence on both personal social systems and institutions, difficulty in participating in treatment on a consistent basis, and difficulty in taking responsibility for the consequences of behavior. At one site, two of the clinical case managers also led an educational group on the effects of street drugs and alcohol on psychiatric condition and discussed ways to prevent relapse. The group served primarily as a means of persuading clients to stop using and engage in more active treatment. All clients also received standard mental health care consisting of individual or group assessment of symptoms and counseling, medication review visits, and minimal case management to stabilize them in the community.

All participating staff were licensed or accredited to provide mental health treatment. One-third of the mental health staff participating had professional certification, experience in alcohol and drug abuse treatment, or both, and many staff had additional training in treating dually diagnosed clients. Mental health center staff in each model chose which model they would implement before the study began and met to discuss implementation, training, and consultation regarding their chosen model. Behavioral skills groups were taught by the same staff at three of the five sites due to a shortage of available personnel; similarly, at two sites, staff jointly conducted mock AA meetings.

Implementation of the three interventions was not smooth, and implementation factors probably relate to client outcomes in the project (Ridgely and Jerrell, in press). For example, in the behavioral skills model, staff adhered to the structured manuals to varying degrees; closer adherence to the prescribed treatment and time frames for the skills groups, augmented somewhat with other group techniques to maintain client motivation, may have produced the most favorable client changes because more skills were learned and reinforced. The greatest fidelity to the original interventions was achieved by staff who were trained in Los Angeles by the developers of the SILS interventions and who had an opportunity to lead groups as part of their training. These staff then led groups across participating mental health centers during the study and helped minimize deviation from the specified model over time. In the case management model, there was variation in terms of whether teams or individual case managers offered the service, the size of the existing mental health service caseloads, the number of clients on these caseloads also receiving substance disorder treatment, and the presence or absence of a group intervention focused on education about drug and alcohol use. Any of these differences may have affected the ability of the case managers either to address alcohol and drug abuse or to provide intensive or specific services that would affect outcomes. There were two significant ways in which the twelve-step programs varied, which may have been related to their effectiveness with clients: the presence or absence of a specific attempt to link to community AA groups through group attendance of community AA, and the recruitment and direct involvement of AA sponsors in the demonstration program. To the extent that these variations increased the AA attendance of clients and their participation in the twelve-step process, clients might demonstrate improved outcomes. As in the typical clinical situation, clinicians and clinical managers chose to balance fidelity to the innovation they were testing with client needs and clinicians' perceptions of what adaptations were necessary.

Implementation was also affected by the extent to which clinical supervisors were perceived as being supportive of the specialized interventions and knowledgeable about the needs of the dually diagnosed target group. At centers where staff felt supported, they provided more service and more intensive service to these clients and had somewhat smaller caseloads to offset the higher acuity and severity of these clients.

## Study Methods

In this study, persons with severe mental illness (DSM-III-R Axis I diagnosis of psychotic or major affective disorder) and with a co-occurring substance disorder who had undergone psychiatric treatment in an inpatient or skilled nursing psychiatric facility or nonhospital residential treatment program (twenty-four-hour locked or acute diversion facility) at least once prior to being referred were the primary target group. In addition referred clients also had to meet at least two of these additional criteria: poor work history over the previous two years; eligibility for and receipt of public assistance; poor basic living skills; poor social support maintenance including a marked inability to establish or maintain a personal support system of family, friends, or co-workers; and a history of exhibiting inappropriate social behavior that resulted in intervention by the mental health or criminal justice systems. The final sample consisted of 132 clients. Seventy-five percent were male, 70 percent were white, 76 percent were diagnosed with schizophrenia, 52 percent were between the ages of 18 and 33, and 48 percent had been hospitalized in the six months prior to entering the study. Most of the clients who were not hospitalized in the six months prior to the referral were either homeless or incarcerated. Referrals were screened, interviewed, and assigned to one of the three intervention approaches.

All clients being served prior to study entry in an existing treatment team or by a solo practitioner were referred to the specialized substance abuse service offered by their treatment team or by clinicians within their agencies (three sites). These teams and clinicians chose which model of substance abuse intervention they would implement. Caseloads for these existing teams or individual clinicians were compared to identify baseline differences on any of the variables employed to balance the sample: gender, ethnicity, age, diagnosis (schizophrenia versus major affective disorders and other psychotic disorders), and number of days in twenty-four-hour placement during the past year. No baseline differences were found. When additional centers, staff, and clients began participating in the study, the new clients were randomly assigned to one of the three interventions. Various statistical control procedures were employed to ensure that the two cohorts were comparable before the data were pooled for the final analyses. On outcome measures in which the two groups (randomized versus nonrandomized) differed, the randomized group was found to be more impaired.

After informed consent was obtained, clients were interviewed every six months after admission using the Social Adjustment Scale II (SAS II) (Schooler, Weissman, and Hogarty, 1979) and the Role Functioning Scale (RFS) (Green and Gracely, 1987), augmented by several additional questions regarding their perceived involvement in mental health services, their use of drugs and alcohol, their medical condition, and their involvement in the criminal justice system. After obtaining client self-reports on the SAS, trained paraprofessional interviewers rated the level of functioning of each subject on the RFS. Agreement among the raters was monitored on an ongoing basis by having up to four interviewers complete ratings of the level of each subject's functioning at each contact, that is, every six months. The summary score for the RFS was formed by averaging the first four subscale scores across raters. Higher scores on these scales represented higher psychosocial functioning and satisfaction. The interviewers also administered the C-DIS-R program (Blouin, 1991) that scored DSM-III-R criteria and symptom counts for depression, mania, schizophrenia, alcohol, and drug abuse symptoms.

Cost-of-care data were based on both public and private mental health services received. Public mental health treatment costs were retrieved from the mental health authority's management information and billing system. These reports included all funding for staff salaries and program operations costs as well as any overhead rate for which funding was received. Total funding was broken down by type of service functions performed; total funding used to provide each service function was divided by the total amount of service provided for each function to calculate a cost per unit of service for each service function. Amount and costs of treatment provided by private mental health service providers to all research clients were obtained from each of those agencies used by the clients in the study. Costs of treatment services were calculated by collecting the cost per unit of service for each treatment facility used by these clients, whether public or private, for each service function and multiplying this unit cost by total units of service received during a six-month period. The total costs per service function and the total cost of mental health care were tallied for each time period.

## Summary of Findings

A description of the average service costs for each intervention program over time is presented first to illustrate the cost differences among the three interventions. As arrayed in Table 6.1, average costs for acute and subacute mental health services ranged between $3,800 and $9,800 during the baseline period but declined over six months by 35 percent to 69 percent across the three models. By the eighteen-month follow-up period, the average acute and subacute services costs (intensive care) had decreased 67 percent in the twelve-step group and 59 percent in the case management group, but had started to trend upward in the behavioral skills model clients, with only a 16 percent decrease over the baseline period. Patterns of supportive service cost changes indicate that outpatient, case management, and supported housing services increased dramatically in the first six months after program entry and then tapered off somewhat for the twelve-step and behavioral skills groups. Costs for medication visits remained fairly constant over time for all groups. Because

Table 6.1. Changes in Mental Health Service Costs for Three Dual Diagnosis Treatment Programs Across Four Time Periods

| Service Costs | AA/12-Step (N = 39) | | | | Behavioral Skills (N = 48) | | | | Case Management (N = 45) | | | |
|---|---|---|---|---|---|---|---|---|---|---|---|---|
| | Baseline | 6 mos | 12 mos | 18 mos | Baseline | 6 mos | 12 mos | 18 mos | Baseline | 6 mos | 12 mos | 18 mos |
| *Intensive Health Services:* | | | | | | | | | | | | |
| Inpatient | $7,660 | $1,794 | $2,196 | $2,026 | $1,641 | $481 | $495 | $1,428 | $2,860 | $2,127 | $1,563 | $1,275 |
| Skilled nursing | $1,158 | $0 | $159 | $734 | $1,356 | $13 | $0 | $928 | $1,606 | $527 | $707 | $273 |
| Residential | $568 | $1,188 | $384 | $309 | $626 | $582 | $122 | $607 | $701 | $655 | $201 | $585 |
| Emergency | $405 | $228 | $184 | $133 | $195 | $120 | $85 | $243 | $426 | $298 | $157 | $169 |
| Subtotal | $9,791 | $3,210 | $2,923 | $3,202 | $3,818 | $1,196 | $702 | $3,206 | $5,593 | $3,607 | $2,628 | $2,302 |
| Change | | -67.2% | -70.1% | -67.3% | | -68.7% | -81.6% | -16.0% | | -35.5% | -53.0% | -58.8% |
| *Supportive Health Services:* | | | | | | | | | | | | |
| Medication | $724 | $757 | $604 | $610 | $619 | $629 | $575 | $553 | $794 | $672 | $565 | $644 |
| Outpatient | $1,852 | $2,483 | $1,870 | $2,343 | $1,115 | $2,060 | $1,897 | $1,569 | $1,611 | $1,474 | $1,251 | $1,598 |
| Case management | $466 | $1,035 | $602 | $677 | $270 | $444 | $635 | $723 | $506 | $726 | $539 | $518 |
| Housing | $349 | $689 | $485 | $433 | $132 | $249 | $699 | $564 | $460 | $475 | $378 | $463 |
| Family services | $196 | $245 | $189 | $252 | $146 | $83 | $83 | $25 | $237 | $261 | $100 | $109 |
| Partial hospitalization | $0 | $0 | $0 | $0 | $6 | $0 | $0 | $0 | $94 | $0 | $0 | $0 |
| Subtotal | $3,587 | $5,209 | $3,750 | $4,315 | $2,288 | $3,465 | $3,889 | $3,434 | $3,702 | $3,608 | $2,833 | $3,332 |
| Change | | 45.2% | 4.5% | 20.3% | | 51.4% | 70.0% | 50.1% | | -2.5% | -23.5% | -10.0% |
| Total Costs | $13,378 | $8,419 | $6,673 | $7,517 | $6,106 | $4,661 | $4,591 | $6,640 | $9,295 | $7,215 | $5,461 | $5,634 |
| Change | | -37.1% | -50.1% | -43.8% | | -23.7% | -24.8% | 8.7% | | -22.4% | -41.2% | -39.4% |

*Note: N = 132. All costs have been standardized to FY90–91 dollars.*

the twelve-step recovery intervention was oriented toward outpatient mock AA meetings and facilitating attendance at actual local AA meetings (reported as case management), the higher costs in terms of outpatient and case management services are consistent with the way service functions were rendered and reported. The behavioral skills groups also were reported primarily as outpatient service; the skill reinforcement sessions were reported as case management, thus accounting for the next highest costs in these two service functions in the behavioral skills group. For the case management group, outpatient service costs (for individual and group treatment) declined over time, whereas case management service costs increased initially and tapered off over time. In general, both the twelve-step and the case management models of service reduced total mental health care costs by 20 percent to 50 percent at the end of eighteen months in the study. Reductions for the behavioral skills group were more modest (19 percent and 23 percent at six and twelve months, respectively), primarily because intensive service costs were lower at baseline. These costs then increased during the eighteen-month follow-up period. This picture is incomplete, however, without considering these changes relative to differences in the mix of clients being served and differences in their service utilization costs prior to entering the study.

To relate these cost differences to changes in other outcomes, the presentation now shifts to summarizing five important outcomes and describing the analyses performed to assess differential outcomes across the three interventions and the impact of supportive services on these outcomes. The critical outcomes are the total SAS II score based on client self-reports every six months, the total RFS score based on the independent raters' observations every six months, the total psychiatric symptoms (schizophrenia, mania, and depression), the total substance abuse symptoms (drug and alcohol), and the total intensive service costs (inpatient, skilled nursing, and residential treatment) that were targeted for reduction by instituting the dual-diagnosis treatment programs. (More detailed presentations regarding psychosocial functioning outcomes are made in Jerrell and Ridgely, 1995a, 1995b.)

To compare differences in psychosocial functioning, symptomatology, and intensive service costs over time statistically, multivariate regression analyses were performed using the total SAS II and RFS scores, total psychiatric and substance abuse symptoms, and the intensive mental health service costs as the outcome or dependent variables. Each experimental program (case management and behavioral skills compared to the twelve-step recovery control condition), each time period (six, twelve, and eighteen months after treatment entry), and the total supportive mental health service costs offered by each dual-diagnosis program to achieve client stabilization and improved functioning (that is, case management hours, outpatient visits, medication visits, supported housing, and day treatment services) were all used as predictor variables to assess differences between the substance disorder intervention approaches and changes over time. These analyses also incorporated each of the variables on which the sample had been balanced, as potentially important aspects of client differences, that is, gender, ethnicity, age, diagnosis, and total twenty-four-hour care days in the six months prior to entry into the program. This was done because previous studies of severely mentally ill clients have shown that men respond differently to treatment than women, younger persons may be harder to stabilize than older clients, persons with schizophrenia may respond differently than those with major affective disorders, nonwhites may respond differently than whites, and so on. In the regressions, shown in Table 6.2, each of these variables is dichotomized and the group listed in the first column is compared to the group in the dichotomy that is not listed (males versus females, whites versus nonwhites, younger versus older, and so on.).

In each analysis (each column of the table), the beta coefficient (first number in each row) indicates not only the difference in that outcome variable related to the predictor variable but also the direction of the difference compared to the dimension of the variable left out of the regression equation, that is, the program serving as the control group (twelve-step recovery), the six months before clients entered the study (baseline), women, nonwhites, diagnoses other than schizophrenia, and clients aged thirty-five years or more. The $t$ value for each variable is also listed in parentheses and an asterisk beside the $t$ value indicates the degree of statistical significance.

The overall self-reported social adjustment (total SAS II score, second column of Table 6.2) was higher for both the behavioral skills and case management models, but not at a statistically significant level ($\beta = 2.17$, $t = 1.92$; $\beta = 1.98$, $t = 1.77$; respectively) compared to the twelve-step recovery model. SAS II scores increased most at six months following program entry and then tapered off at twelve and eighteen months. Overall role functioning as rated by trained interviewers (total RFS score, third column) was higher for the behavioral skills group than for either of the other two groups ($\beta = .57$ and $t = 1.32$), but not at a statistically significant level. There were significant increases in observed role functioning over time at six months ($\beta = 1.60$ and $t = 3.58$), twelve months ($\beta = 2.15$ and $t = 4.78$), and eighteen months ($\beta = 2.12$ and $t = 4.17$), compared to the six months prior to entry into the specialized substance abuse service programs. Providing more mental health supportive services (as indicated by higher-than-average supportive service costs) was significantly correlated with increases in self-reported social adjustment ($\beta = 3.22$ and $t = 3.33$) and in observed role functioning ($\beta = 1.01$ and $t = 2.73$).

Also important to an evaluation of the impact of these substance disorder interventions are data regarding changes in self-reported psychiatric and substance abuse symptoms. Total psychiatric symptom counts were significantly lower for both the case management and behavioral skills groups than for the twelve-step group. However, only the behavioral skills group clients reported significantly lower total substance abuse symptoms. Over time, both psychiatric and substance abuse symptoms were reduced, but not to a statistically significant degree except for substance abuse symptoms at the eighteen-month follow-up. There was no association between the amount of supportive service costs and decreased reports of symptomatology.

**Table 6.2.    Factors Related to Social Adjustment, Role Functioning, Symptomatology, and Mental Health Service Costs**

| Predictors | SAS Summary Score | RFS Summary Score | Total Psychiatric Symptoms | Total Drug and Alcohol Symptoms | Intensive MH Costs ($) | Supportive MH Costs ($) |
|---|---|---|---|---|---|---|
| Case management | 1.98[a] | 0.03 | −5.08 | 0.45 | −1167 | −997 |
| | (1.77)[b] | (0.08) | (5.17)** | (0.55) | (1.35) | (2.52)* |
| Behavioral skills | 2.17 | 0.57 | −5.04 | −2.29 | −1855 | −939 |
| | (1.92) | (1.32) | (5.11)** | (2.79)** | (2.13)* | (2.35)* |
| Male | −1.11 | −2.21 | −2.09 | 0.25 | −461 | 469 |
| | (1.07) | (5.53)** | (2.30)* | (0.33) | (0.57) | (1.25) |
| White | 1.77 | 1.25 | −1.45 | −0.54 | 319 | 1583 |
| | (1.79) | (3.30)** | (1.65) | (0.74) | (0.42) | (4.56)** |
| Age 18–33 | 0.70 | −0.67 | 1.03 | 0.37 | 146 | 119 |
| | (0.78) | (1.96)* | (1.31) | (0.57) | (0.21) | (0.37) |
| Schizophrenia | −1.07 | −0.70 | 0.40 | 0.00 | −1205 | 1139 |
| | (0.98) | (1.69) | (0.42) | (0.00) | (2.81)** | (2.90)** |
| Prior hospitalization | −2.57 | −1.55 | −0.43 | −0.71 | 5193 | 86 |
| | (2.76)** | (4.35)** | (0.53) | (1.05) | (7.25)** | (0.26) |
| High supportive costs | 3.22 | 1.01 | 0.39 | −0.12 | −2114 | |
| | (3.33)** | (2.73)** | (0.46) | (0.18) | (2.82)** | |
| 6 months | 2.15 | 1.60 | −1.42 | −0.93 | −3431 | 875 |
| | (1.83) | (3.58)** | (1.38) | (1.08) | (3.74)** | (2.05)* |
| 12 months | 1.27 | 2.15 | −0.66 | −0.53 | −4105 | 316 |
| | (1.09) | (4.78)** | (0.64) | (0.62) | (4.47)** | (0.74) |
| 18 months | 0.90 | 2.12 | −1.84 | −2.14 | −3009 | 459 |
| | (0.68) | (4.17)** | (1.57) | (2.21)* | (3.04)** | (0.99) |
| Constant | 73.47 | 12.87 | 18.10 | 7.32 | 6381 | 1406 |
| | (39.46)** | (18.06)** | (11.08)** | (5.39)** | (4.42)** | (2.10)* |
| $R^2$ | 0.08 | 0.22 | 0.11 | 0.04 | 0.19 | 0.08 |
| Mean | 75.86 | 12.42 | 11.87 | 5.50 | 3471 | 3582 |
| F | 3.62** | 11.94** | 4.91** | 1.78 | 10.43** | 4.22** |

[a] $\beta$ coefficient
[b] $t$ value
\* Significant at $p \le .05$
\*\* Significant at $p \le .01$

In the final outcome, the costs of intensive acute and subacute mental health service utilization for these dually diagnosed clients were significantly lower for the behavioral skills model ($\beta = -1,855$ and $t = 2.13$) than for the other two intervention approaches. This difference was evident throughout the study period, however, and no differential reduction favoring the behavioral skills group was evident in further analyses. Intensive service costs were slightly lower for the case management model but not to a statistically significant degree. Over the duration of the program, the costs of intensive mental health services were significantly reduced compared to the six months prior to program entry. Providing more supportive mental health services for these clients was significantly associated with reduced intensive service costs.

Supportive service costs were significantly lower for both the case management and behavioral skills models than for the twelve-step model, and although these costs increased significantly during the first six months after program entry, they tapered off thereafter. Over time and across all treatment groups, the total intensive and supportive mental health care costs were, on average, about $14,000 per client annually.

In summary, statistically significant differences favoring the behavioral skills model were evident on two of the major outcome variables: reductions in psychiatric symptoms and drug and alcohol symptoms. On two other outcomes, self-reported psychosocial adjustment and interviewer ratings of functioning, the main difference favored the behavioral skills model but not to a statistically significant degree. Providing more supportive services was significantly correlated with enhanced functioning and with reduced intensive mental health service costs. Across most of the outcome variables, change occurred at different times.

## Conclusions and Implications for Clinical Care

In conclusion, these results should reinforce the efforts of clinicians to provide specialized treatments to clients with dual disorders aimed at treating both disorders simultaneously. The effectiveness of these efforts can be documented in systematic studies, and persons with severe mental illness can be stabilized and their functioning enhanced through the provision of these treatments. The provision of specialized treatments aimed at both the mental health and the substance problems not only stabilizes clients with dual disorders in community-based, supportive services but over time the total cost of caring for these clients decreases as well. On some outcome indicators, the amount of supportive service resources invested correlates with enhanced functioning and lower intensive (acute and subacute) service costs.

In order to obtain this type of understanding of the effectiveness and relative costs of promising interventions, however, more studies of such alternatives are needed. Comparisons of both the costs and effectiveness of alternative approaches are most useful in current practice settings because intervention models that achieve noteworthy effects may not be the least costly. Within the managed care environment, such alternatives may be short-lived. It is therefore important to investigate both the cost and the effectiveness of interventions to fully appreciate their relative value in practice.

These results indicate that outcomes for clients in the behavioral skills model were more positive on indicators of psychosocial functioning and symptom reductions than either of the other two interventions. Thus, interventions that address the cognitive and behavioral deficits that these clients have are important aspects of their active treatment for both psychiatric and substance abuse problems, even when some of the skills are not specifically related to substance abuse. Although the case management model also demonstrated some positive effects on client outcomes, it might have more impact when used in conjunction with a more structured, active substance abuse treatment component. Because there are no other studies of dual-diagnosis interventions to compare these results to, it is difficult to draw any further conclusions from these data. Hopefully they will stimulate more work on this topic that will be useful in clinical practice.

Although these results represent the most comprehensive assessment of interventions for dual-disorder clients to date, there are certain limitations that remain to be addressed in future studies. In the target population for this study, clients with pronounced personality disorders were excluded even though personality disorders are highly correlated with substance disorders. These results should not be generalized beyond the severely mentally ill target group in this study. Additional work is needed to examine interventions for clients with psychotic, characterological, and substance disorders. Furthermore, although a totally randomized design would have yielded stronger scientific conclusions, the incorporation of existing teams and individual caseloads bolsters the generalizability of the results to actual practice. And finally, there are many other approaches to treating substance disorders and variations on model approaches that still need to be studied for clinicians and clinical managers to obtain a better understanding of what approaches work most efficiently and effectively with dual-disorder clients. Rather than being definitive, these results should point to areas in which clinicians and clinical program managers can be active partners with services researchers in identifying and investigating promising interventions for dual-disorder clients and promoting more cost-effective regular care.

## References

Barbee, J., Clark, P., Crapanzano, M., Heintz, G. C., and Kehoe, C. E. "Alcohol and Substance Abuse Among Schizophrenic Patients Presenting to an Emergency Service." *Journal of Nervous and Mental Disease*, 1989, *177*, 400–407.

Bartels, S. J., Teague, G. B., Drake, R. E., Clark, R. E., Bush, P. W., and Noordsy, D. L. "Substance Abuse in Schizophrenia: Service Utilization and Costs." *Journal of Nervous and Mental Disease*, 1993, *181* (4), 227–232.

Bassuk, E. "The Impact of Deinstitutionalization on the General Psychiatric Emergency Ward." *Hospital and Community Psychiatry*, 1980, *31*, 623–627.

Blouin, A. "Computer-Based Diagnostic Interview Schedule Revised." Toronto: C-DIS Management Group, 1991.

Caton, C. "The New Chronic Patient and the System of Community Care." *Hospital and Community Psychiatry*, 1981, *32*, 475–488.

Chen, C., Balogh, M., Bathija, J., Howanitz, E., Plutchik, R., and Conte, H. R. "Substance Abuse Among Psychiatric Inpatients." *Comprehensive Psychiatry*, 1992, *33*, 60–64.

Eckman, T., Liberman, R. P., Phipps, C., and Blair, K. "Teaching Medication Management Skills to Schizophrenic Patients." *Journal of Clinical Psychopharmacology*, 1990, *10*, 33–38.

Green, R., and Gracely, E. "Selecting a Rating Scale for Evaluating Services to the Chronically Mentally Ill." *Community Mental Health Journal*, 1987, *23*, 91–102.

Jerrell, J. M., and Ridgely, M. S. "Comparative Effectiveness of Three Approaches to Serving People with Severe Mental Illness and Substance Abuse Disorders." *Journal of Nervous and Mental Disorders*, 1995a, *183*, 566–576.

Jerrell, J. M., and Ridgely, M. S. "Evaluating Changes in Symptoms and Functioning of Dually Diagnosed Clients in Specialized Treatment." *Psychiatric Services*, 1995b, *46* (3), 233–238.

Kessler, R. C., McGonagle, K. A., Zhao, S., Nelson, C. B., Hughes, M., Eshleman, S., Wittchen, H., and Kendler, K. S. "Lifetime and Twelve-Month Prevalence of DSM-III-R Psychiatric Disorders in the United States." *Archives of General Psychiatry*, 1994, *51*, 8–19.

Liberman, R. P., Massel, H., Mosk, M., and Wong, S. "Social Skills Training for Chronic Mental Patient." *Hospital and Community Psychiatry*, 1985, *36*, 396–403.

Lyons, J., and McGovern, M. "Use of Mental Health Services by Dually Diagnosed Patients." *Hospital and Community Psychiatry*, 1989, *40*, 1067–1069.

Richardson, M., Craig, T., and Haughland, G. "Treatment Patterns of Young Chronic Schizophrenic Patients in the Era of Deinstitutionalization." *Psychiatric Quarterly*, 1985, *57*, 243–249.

Ridgely, M. S., and Jerrell, J. M. "Analysis of Three Interventions for Substance Abuse Treatment of Severely Mentally Ill People." *Community Mental Health Journal*, 1995, in press.

Safer, D. "Substance Abuse by Young Adult Chronic Patients." *Hospital and Community Psychiatry*, 1987, *38*, 511–514.

Schooler, N., Weissman, M., and Hogarty, G. "Social Adjustment Scale for Schizophrenics." In W. A. Hargreaves, C. C. Attkisson, and J. Sorenson (eds.), *Resource Material for Community Mental Health Program Evaluators*. DHHS pub. no. (ADM) 79328. Rockville, Md.: National Institute of Mental Health, 1979.

Solomon, P. "Receipt of Aftercare Services by Problem Types: Psychiatric, Psychiatric/Substance Abuse, and Substance Abuse." *Psychiatric Quarterly*, 1986, *58*, 180–188.

*JEANETTE M. JERRELL, Ph.D., is professor of neuropsychiatry and behavioral science at the School of Medicine, University of South Carolina.*

*Research on the prevalence, patterns, and course of substance use disorders in severe mental illness gives key insights into the complex interaction of substance use and mental disorder. Understanding the literature on comorbidity has implications for the design of clinical services and for the direction of future research in the field.*

# Comorbid Substance Use Disorder: Prevalence, Patterns of Use, and Course

*Brian J. Cuffel*

Problems in the assessment, diagnosis, and treatment of persons with severe mental illnesses and comorbid substance use disorders have long been recognized by mental health professionals and others observing public mental health systems (Bachrach, 1982; Bergman and Harris, 1985; Pepper, Kirshner, and Ryglewicz, 1981). In part these problems reflect a lack of understanding of the nature of substance disorders as they occur in persons with severe mental illness and how comorbid substance disorders interact with mental disorder to influence symptoms, functioning, and course of treatment.

Until recently, clinical observation and anecdotal reports of key informants were the main source of information about the clinical needs of persons with severe mental illness. Now a growing body of empirical research addresses many of these clinical impressions and provides key insights into the nature and complexity of substance use disorders in this population. Although many questions remain unanswered, empirical research is accumulating regarding three important questions: What is the extent of substance use disorder in severe mental illness and what are the most prevalently abused substances? What are the most frequently occurring patterns of substance use disorders and what are their clinical implications? What is the time course of substance use disorders, including the consequences of continued abuse and the benefits of substance use reduction?

In this chapter, empirical research on each question is reviewed to guide the development of more effective and targeted clinical programs and to direct efforts toward areas in need of more research. Perhaps more importantly, this

New Directions for Mental Health Services, no. 70, Summer 1996 © Jossey-Bass Publishers research furthers our understanding of the etiology and interaction of substance use and mental disorder.

## Prevalence of Comorbid Substance Use Disorder

Debate about the extent of substance use disorders in schizophrenia and other severe mental illnesses has important etiologic and clinical implications (Cuffel, 1992). Early reviews of the literature cited wide-ranging prevalence estimates for a variety of substance use disorders. At the time, it was suggested that persons with schizophrenia were at no greater risk for alcohol, cannabis, and opiate disorders than the general population but were at greater risk for stimulant and hallucinogen disorders (Mueser and others, 1990; Schneier and Siris, 1987). These reviews were used to support the notion that persons with schizophrenia preferentially used stimulants to elevate their mood, to self-medicate negative symptoms, or to alleviate the side effects of their neuroleptic treatment. These conclusions have been challenged and revised by published estimates of the rates of comorbidity in large epidemiologic samples (Kessler and others, 1994; Regier and others, 1990) and by more rigorous reviews of the literature that show that the highest rates of alcohol and other substance use disorders occur in persons with schizophrenia and bipolar disorder (Cuffel, 1992; Mueser, Bellack, and Blanchard, 1992; Mueser, Bennett, and Kushner, 1995).

**Large-Scale Community Surveys.** The best data come from two large epidemiologic studies of mental disorder in the United States. NIMH's Epidemiologic Catchment Area (EMA) study indicates that the lifetime prevalence of alcohol disorder is highest in bipolar (46.2 percent) and schizophrenic disorders (33.7 percent) and elevated relative to the general population (16.7 percent), other affective disorders (21.8 percent), and anxiety disorders (17.9 percent) (Regier and others, 1990). A similar pattern of results is observed for drug disorders in the ECA study with the highest rates in persons with schizophrenia and bipolar disorder. Results from NIMH's National Comorbidity Study (NCS) may offer a replication of the ECA findings, although no results regarding schizophrenia or bipolar disorder are available at the time of this writing. The National Comorbidity Study has reported on the comorbidity of alcohol abuse and dependence with anxiety and affective disorders. Lifetime NCS rates are considerably higher than those reported in the ECA study finding rates of abuse and dependence exceeding 50 percent for both affective and anxiety disorders (Crum and others, 1995).

**Quantitative Review of the Prevalence Literature.** The predominance of alcohol disorders in schizophrenia is also supported by reviews of the comorbidity literature (Cuffel, 1992; Mueser, Bellack, and Blanchard, 1992). A quantitative review conducted by Cuffel in 1992 identified thirteen studies reporting the prevalence of alcohol abuse and dependence and nine studies reporting the prevalence of stimulant abuse and dependence. Results suggested that prevalence estimates were strongly correlated with the year in which the data were collected ($r$ = .62 in the case of alcohol abuse and dependence and $r$ = .73 for stimulus abuse and dependence) with more recent studies showing the highest rates of alcohol and stimulant abuse. Estimates placed the rate of alcohol abuse and dependence in schizophrenia at 40 percent and the rates of stimulant abuse at 19 percent.

A reanalysis of the alcohol prevalence publication trends, including studies published since 1991, was conducted to examine the consistency of alcohol prevalence rates with past research and to determine whether the findings of the earlier review are consistent with recently published literature. Since 1991, five studies reporting the prevalence of alcohol and other substance use disorders have been published that meet the criteria of my earlier quantitative review. Studies were reviewed if they had at least fifteen subjects, specified the number of subjects in each diagnostic group that abused and did not abuse substances, and did not preferentially select subjects with a history of substance abuse (Duke, Pantelis, and Barnes, 1994; Mueser, Yarnold, and Bellack, 1992; Rosenthal, Hellerstein, and Miner, 1992; Shaner and others, 1993; Stone, Greenstein, Gamble, and McLellan, 1993). Again, alcohol abuse rates in recently published studies are consistently high in persons with schizophrenia. Although the debate about whether or not alcohol rates are actually increasing in persons with schizophrenia cannot be resolved from these data alone, it is clear that more recent studies find rates of alcohol abuse that exceed 40 percent. Compounding the difficulty of comparing prevalence rates over time is the fact that the sensitivity of substance assessment is method-dependent (Drake, Alterman, and Rosenberg, 1993; Drake and Wallach, 1989). More recent studies may yield higher and more accurate estimates because they use multiple sources of information, structured research interviews, and diagnostic criteria.

**Implications of Current Prevalence Findings.** Widely available substances such as alcohol, cannabis, and stimulants are the most widely abused substances in persons with severe mental illness. The notion that differences in symptoms, subjective experience, and treatment of psychiatric conditions lead to differences in substance use preferences has been the focus of research and debate on the prevalence of comorbid substance use disorders. Earlier studies of the prevalence of alcohol and other substance disorders in schizophrenia were taken as evidence of differential substance preferences in various diagnostic groups and consequently were used as support for self-medication theories of substance use disorders (Schneier and Siris, 1987). In particular, lower-than-expected rates of alcohol abuse and higher-than-expected rates of stimulant and hallucinogen abuse were used as evidence that persons with schizophrenia use certain drugs to alleviate negative symptoms of schizophrenia or to mitigate the side effects of neuroleptic treatment.

Undoubtedly, substance disorder is multiply determined and affected by social, environmental, biological, and psychological factors in the lives of persons with severe mental illness. However, the notion of a specific symptom-substance connection, as suggested in some self-medication theories of substance abuse, is no longer supported by the data on comorbidity. The evidence is more consistent with the notion that severe mental disorder affects the manifestation of substance use disorder more broadly by increasing persons' vulnerabilities to a wide variety of substances. Specific substance choice may be more affected by factors such as sociodemographics, substance availability and cost, and social and peer influences. Current research has turned to understanding the more complex and intriguing problem of the interactive effects of substance use and mental disorders.

## Patterns of Substance Abuse in Severe Mental Illness

Motivated by the need to understand the interaction of mental and substance disorders and to make accurate and clinically useful assessments of comorbid substance use disorders, investigators have begun to study the patterns and heterogeneity of substance use disorders across diagnostic conditions. Substance use disorders are not homogeneously manifested in persons with severe mental illness even within specific categories. Variation within and across primary and secondary mental disorders appears to have implications for assessment, treatment planning, and for understanding the nature of the substance disorder–mental disorder interaction.

**Patterns of Substance Use Disorders.** The most recent and well-designed research compares substance use disorders between groups whose mental disorder is primary versus secondary to substance use disorder. Lehman has described the importance of this distinction and his empirical work provides evidence that substance use disorders manifest themselves differently when they co-occur with a primary mental disorder than when they occur with a secondary mental disorder or alone (Lehman, Myers, and Corty, 1989; Lehman, Myers, Corty, and Thompson, 1994). Using the Structured Clinical Interview for DSMIII-R (SCID) and clinical records in an inpatient setting, patients were assigned to one of three groups: Independent Mental Disorder and Primary Substance Use Disorder (IMD+PSUD), Primary Substance-Induced Organic Mental Disorder (PSUD-OMD), and PSUD only.

Comparison of patients in the IMD+PSUD, PSUD-OMD, and PSUD groups found that those with IMD+PSUD have significantly fewer severe substance use disorder problems (Lehman, Myers, Corty, and Thompson, 1994). With the exception of alcohol disorders, substance use disorder severity ratings were lower in PSUD than in the other substance use disorder groups and persons with IMD+PSUD were significantly less likely to abuse hardcore street drugs such as opiates, cocaine, and polysubstances. Instead they were more likely to abuse what Lehman refers to as *entry-level* substances such as alcohol and cannabis.

Lehman's findings are somewhat surprising given the documented vulnerability of persons with many mental disorders to substance abuse, although they are consistent with earlier research showing that the presence of a primary mental disorder (other than antisocial personality disorder) is associated with lower severity of alcohol-related symptoms (Cook, Winokur, and Fowler, 1994; Alterman, Ayre, and Williford, 1984). The findings are not consistent with the notion that persons with schizophrenia preferentially abuse stimulant and hallucinogenic drugs, which suggests that these drugs are less often the drugs of choice for this population.

The primacy of alcohol and cannabis disorders in persons with severe mental illness is underscored by research that examines the naturally occurring patterns of lifetime substance use disorders in schizophrenia (Cuffel, Heithoff, and Lawson, 1993). Using a multivariate technique for categorical data referred to as latent class analysis, two patterns of lifetime substance use disorder were identified in persons receiving a Diagnostic Interview Schedule diagnosis of schizophrenia in the ECA study. The technique, analogous to factor analysis, constructs underlying classes of variables that empirically account for the observed pattern of co-occurrences among categorical variables.

Consistent with the Lehman findings, the most prevalent latent class of abuse was characterized by high levels of alcohol and cannabis abuse with little or no use of other types of illicit substances (31 percent). Persons with this pattern of abuse appear to be highly likely to abuse both alcohol and cannabis. Interestingly, lifetime abuse of alcohol or cannabis in isolation was rare. The second, less prevalent pattern involves pervasive substance use including high rates of alcohol and cannabis disorders but also high rates of stimulant, hallucinogen, opiate, and sedative disorders. Comprising 14 percent of the sample, persons in the latter group had developed problematic use of several substances and were indistinguishable from the group that used alcohol and cannabis alone in terms of sociodemographics, age of onset, rate of psychotic and depressive symptoms, and rate of psychiatric emergency and hospital service use.

Both substance-disordered groups were more likely to be male, younger, and have higher levels of depressive symptoms than the group without substance disorder problems. The results are not consistent with a unique symptom–substance association; nor do they suggest that certain drug use patterns are more likely to lead to depression. Emerging evidence suggests that persons with schizophrenia and multiple substance use are more likely to evidence violent and destructive behaviors in the community, however (Bartels, Drake, Wallach, and Freeman, 1991; Cuffel, Shumway, Chouljian, and MacDonald, 1994).

**Heterogeneity of Substance Use Disorders Across Diagnoses.** The most methodologically demanding studies of comorbid substance use disorder examine the heterogeneity of substance use disorders across specific diagnostic conditions. Most studies include only persons in treatment or presenting for treatment and these samples may demonstrate biased presentations of symptoms (Shumway and Cuffel, in press). In addition, few studies have sufficiently large samples to permit comparison across different diagnostic categories; most group all mental disorders together or focus on a single diagnostic group.

One published study used ECA data to overcome these deficiencies. Shumway and Cuffel (in press) studied whether diagnostic subgroups are associated with distinct patterns of alcohol-related signs and symptoms. Lifetime symptoms of persons with alcohol disorder alone were compared to symptoms of persons with alcohol disorder and the following DSM-III diagnostic categories: antisocial personality disorder, schizophrenia, affective disorder, and anxiety disorder. Subjects were individuals who met criteria for alcohol dependence and abuse in their lifetimes ($n = 1955$).

Different patterns of alcohol-related symptoms distinguished each of the comorbid groups from the groups with alcohol disorder alone. Persons with comorbid schizophrenic disorders were significantly more likely than persons with alcohol disorder alone to engage in chronic heavy drinking; to become involved in physical fights; to report that others, such as physicians and friends, objected to their drinking; and to experience withdrawal symptoms. The expression of alcohol disorder noted in persons with schizophrenia was similar in some ways to persons with antisocial personality disorder, who also reported problems with physical fights while drinking. The alcohol disorders of persons with antisocial personality disorder, however, also showed earlier age of onset, more binges and benders, and more legal problems associated with drinking while driving and alcohol-related arrests. Persons with antisocial personality disorder were less likely to report family objections to their drinking.

**Implications of Patterns of Substance Use Disorder.** The empirical research on subtypes, heterogeneity, and patterns of comorbidity help to dispel the myth of the typical dual-diagnosis patient (Weiss, Mirin, and Frances, 1992). Research to date is important in what it suggests about how substance use disorders are expressed in persons with severe mental illness and how comorbid substance use disorders differ from primary substance use disorders. First, drug disorders co-occurring with psychiatric disorders may be less prevalent and less severe than drug-use disorders occurring alone. Second, despite apparently lower severity, alcohol disorders in schizophrenia may be associated with higher rates of social and behavioral consequences. Third, a pattern of multiple substance use disorders has been identified in persons with schizophrenia that includes a significant minority of the dually diagnosed. Although demographically and symptomatically similar to persons who abuse only alcohol and cannabis, persons who exhibit comorbid polysubstance use may be more difficult and costly to manage in outpatient settings and may evidence higher rates of violence (Cuffel, Shumway, Chouljian, and MacDonald, 1994). The fact that certain substances such as cocaine are rarely abused alone presents problems for research on the correlates of comorbid substance abuse. Previous research on the correlates of substance use disorders in persons with severe mental illness has been problematic because it has ignored the confounding influences of polysubstance abuse. Future studies in the area must be cognizant of polysubstance abuse in their samples before making inferences based on the correlates of single substances.

## Course of Substance Use Disorders
## in Severe Mental Illness

Perhaps the greatest need is for longitudinal data on the nature and severity of substance use disorders in persons with severe mental illness. We are only beginning to address questions related to the persistence and temporal stability of substance use disorders in this population and the effect of changing substance use status on the treatment, clinical course, and quality of life of persons with severe mental illness.

The vast majority of research to date has been cross-sectional and has been well reviewed by Mueser, Bellack, and Blanchard (1992). Most studies agree that substance-abusing persons with schizophrenia tend to be young males of low socioeconomic status (Drake, Osher, and Wallach, 1989; Drake and Wallach, 1989; Mueser and others, 1990). Their backgrounds tend to show fewer prior hospitalizations (Mueser and others, 1990), more stable premorbid personalities (Dixon and others, 1991; Turner and Tsuang, 1990), and more frequent family histories of drug abuse (Tsuang, Simpson, and Kronfol, 1982). Comorbidity is associated with more problems in obtaining meals, managing finances, and maintaining stable housing (Drake, Osher, and Wallach, 1989; Drake and Wallach, 1989). Some studies have found increased levels of hostility, depression, violence, suicide, and management problems in the hospital, community, and at home (Alterman, Erdlen, McLellan, and Mann, 1980; Alterman, Erdlen, and Murphy, 1981; McCarrick, Manderscheid, and Bertolucci, 1985; Sevy, Kay, Opler, and van Praag, 1990). Despite apparently greater psychosocial and functioning deficits, persons with comorbid substance use disorder and schizophrenia may not be more symptomatic and their response to antipsychotic treatment may be equivalent to or better than persons without comorbid substance use disorders (Buckley, Thompson, Way, and Meltzer, 1994; Dixon and others, 1991).

The absence of longitudinal studies, however, limits our ability to make definitive statements about the causal role of substance use disorders in severe mental illness. As a result, our ability to inform mental health providers, families, and community members about the potential effects of substance use disorders on severe mental illness and the potential benefits of substance use disorder remission is limited.

What we have learned to date comes from a handful of studies of the changes in substance use disorders over time and the clinical correlates of these changes. These studies indicate that without intensive targeted interventions, substance use disorders have a high likelihood of persisting and may have deleterious effects on treatment outcome, functioning, and quality of life.

Five studies reporting rates of remission and relapse of substance disorders in persons with severe mental illness have been reported in the literature (Bartels, Drake, and Wallach, 1995; Cuffel and Chase, 1994; Drake, McHugo, and Noordsy, 1993; Drake and Wallach, 1993; Ries and Ellingson, 1990).

In the longest prospective follow-up study published to date, Bartels and others (1995) followed a cohort of persons with severe mental illness being treated by a mobile community-based ambulatory service team for a period of seven years. Using the Case Manager Rating Scale, substance use disorder status was rated according to DSM-III-R categories. Ratings were made by the patient's case manager for the period six months prior to the baseline and seven-year follow-up interviews.

Rates of substance use in the Bartels, Drake, and Wallach cohort were constant over time, suggesting that substance use disorder overall in this sample showed no general trends. Although the prevalence of alcohol and other drug disorders in the cohort were unchanged over the seven-year period, considerable variation was observed in the substance use status of individuals. The remission rate for persons with alcohol abuse at baseline was 67 percent. Remission of alcohol dependence was considerably lower at 33 percent. An alarming 41 percent of those meeting criteria for alcohol dependence at baseline remained dependent at seven-year follow-up. It is noteworthy that few persons with schizophrenia were able to maintain "moderate drinking" levels at baseline. Over half of moderate drinkers became abstinent during the seven-year period and nearly a quarter developed an alcohol disorder problem at seven-year follow-up (Drake and Wallach, 1993). Estimates from this research suggest that no more than one in five individuals drinks moderately as a long-term drinking pattern.

The remission rate for persons with other drug abuse was 54 percent in the Bartels, Drake, and Wallach cohort. Again, remission of drug dependence was considerably lower than that for abuse at 31 percent. However, compared to persons with alcohol dependence at baseline, fewer persons with drug dependence disorders remained dependent at seven-year follow-up (25 percent), suggesting that this level of drug use is less often maintained over extended periods of time. Instead, persons with severe mental illness appeared much more likely to lower their drug use from dependence to abuse.

The findings of the seven year follow-up by Bartels, Drake, and Wallach are consistent with the one-year rates of substance use disorder remission and relapse reported by Cuffel and Chase (1994). In the latter study, one-year remission and relapse rates were based on data collected for NIMH's Epidemiologic Catchment Area program. The data are valuable in that they are prospectively collected and come from a community-based sample not identified through a treatment setting. Subjects were the 168 persons who met DSM-III criteria for schizophrenia based on DIS interviews.

Results showed that substance abuse prevalence was constant in schizophrenia over the year and that annual remission and relapse rates counterbalanced to maintain a constant level of substance abuse and dependence in the sample (Cuffel and Chase, 1994). One-year remission rates among those with abuse or dependence at baseline were 31 percent for alcohol and 50 percent for drug abuse and dependence, but were based on small numbers. When the long-term course of substance abuse was simulated using Markov modeling techniques, results indicated that untreated substance use disorders would not decline in this population in the long run.

In contrast, it appears that higher rates of remission and relapse can be achieved using Program for Assertive Community Treatment (PACT) teams (Test, 1992). Longitudinal research reported by Drake, McHugo, and Noordsy found higher rates of remission and lower rates of relapse in a small sample of eighteen patients who were treated in PACT teams (Drake, McHugo, and Noordsy, 1993). PACT teams achieved a 61 percent remission rate at four-year follow-up. This rate compares favorably to the 30 percent to 40 percent remission rates of other studies reported by Bartels, Drake, and Wallach (1995) and Cuffel and Chase (1994). Ries and Ellingson (1990) reported 70 percent remission from substance use disorders in a sample of seventeen dual-diagnosis patients after treatment in a specialized inpatient program. Their one month follow-up interval, however, makes these results difficult to interpret.

**Correlates of Change in Substance Use Disorder.** Longitudinal data on comorbid substance disorders provide compelling support for the notion that changes in substance disorder have significant effects on symptoms, functioning, and quality of life. In the study by Cuffel and Chase, substance disorders were not only associated with depressive symptoms as in past research (Cuffel, Heithoff, and Lawson, 1993; Brady and others, 1990; Sevy, Kay, Opler, and van Praag, 1990), but were also found to co-vary over time. Individuals who developed a new substance disorder reported increases in depression during the year even controlling for prior depressive symptoms. Those who stopped a substance use disorder reported significant relief from depressive symptoms. The pattern exhibited by the latter group strongly suggests that remission of substance use disorders can bring significant reductions in depressive symptoms.

Similarly, development of a new substance use disorder appears to be associated with increased risk for hospitalization (Cuffel and others, 1994; Drake, Osher, and Wallach, 1989). Reductions in substance disorder appear to lower the risk of hospitalization to that of persons who have no history of substance abuse. The longitudinal nature of the Cuffel and Chase (1994) study allows the effects of recent disorder to be partialled from the effects of ongoing use disorders and history of use disorders. Results show that rates of hospitalization among those who developed a new substance use disorder (24 percent) were comparable to rates for those with ongoing substance disorders (21 percent) and much higher than that for those who recently stopped abuse (0 percent) or from those who had been abstinent for some time (6 percent). History of substance abuse or dependence appears to have little effect on risk for hospitalization, and current abuse or dependence appears to determine risk for hospitalization. At least one other study contradicts the conclusion that persons with a history of substance abuse are not at greater risk for hospitalization, however (Kivlahan and others, 1991). Finally, one study has examined retrospective longitudinal data on the relationship between changes in substance disorder status and global functioning in persons with schizophrenia

(Shumway, Chouljian, and Hargreaves, 1994). This study fully exploits its longitudinal data and serves as an analytic model for future longitudinal research in this area. Subjects were one hundred persons receiving SCID diagnoses of schizophrenia, schizoaffective, or schizophreniform disorder and treated in a controlled trial of family interventions for persons with schizophrenia.

Substance use disorder and functional level were rated at three-month intervals from clinical records with good interrater reliability. Time-related changes in substance disorder and functional level were modeled as a stochastic process in order to determine patterns of change consistent with one or both of two causal hypotheses: substance use disorder increases lead to decreases in functional level, and decreases in functional level lead to increases in substance disorder. Support was found for the hypothesis that occurrences of substance disorder more often precede decreases in functional level. The reverse was not found. That is, decreases in functional level followed by increased use of substances were rarely found.

**Implications of Longitudinal Data on Substance Disorders.** The longitudinal data, although scarce, provide the most persuasive evidence for the negative consequences of comorbid disorders on the lives of persons with severe mental illness. Increases in substance use disorder appear to be accompanied by increases in depressive symptoms and hospitalization and decreases in community functioning (Cuffel and Chase, 1994; Shumway, Chouljian, and Hargreaves, 1994). Decreases in substance use appear to provide relief from depressive symptoms and to significantly lower use of psychiatric inpatient care. These are compelling data that mental health care systems for persons with severe mental illness must adopt effective programs that target substance use disorders.

## Conclusions

Empirical research on the epidemiology of psychiatric comorbidity has advanced our understanding of one of the most challenging clinical populations. Not only is the magnitude of substance use disorders now well recognized and empirically documented in a variety of settings but we now have a better understanding of the most problematic substances for persons with severe mental illness.

The next generation of comorbidity research will be faced with the much more difficult task of understanding the etiology, development, and most cost-effective treatments for comorbid disorders. The complex interaction of mood, substance disorder, symptomatology, and functioning warrants further attention, particularly in emerging treatment studies in which changes in one domain can be observed for their effects in others.

As we consider the extent of substance disorders in persons with severe mental illness, another line of research becomes apparent: prevention and early intervention research. Mental health policy makers must consider the case for prevention and early intervention programs targeting substance use disorder in persons with first-break psychoses seen in public and private mental health systems. The challenges of developing and financing any prevention program in the current political and economic environment are formidable. Prevalence data on substance use disorders in schizophrenia and bipolar disorder are so persuasive, however, that the case for prevention programs must now be made.

We can now say that about half of young persons presenting their first episodes of schizophrenia and bipolar disorder will develop a substance use disorder in their lifetime. With little effort, we can increase the predictive value of diagnosis by identifying subgroups of such persons who are at even greater risk for the development of comorbid substance disorders—young males, for example. Given that substance disorders are highly prevalent, complicate and intensify the course of treatment, and have demonstrable effects on functioning and symptomatology, they may appreciably increase costs to the mental health system (Bartels and others, 1993). Prevention of substance use disorders may ultimately be more cost-effective than tertiary interventions for persons with dual diagnoses who are caught up in a cycle of substance abuse, psychosis, community disruption, and emergency room detoxification.

## References

Alterman, A. I., Ayre, F. R., and Williford, W. O. "Diagnostic Validation of Conjoint Schizophrenia and Alcoholism." *Journal of Clinical Psychiatry,* 1984, *45,* 300–303.

Alterman, A. I., Erdlen, F. R., McLellan, A. T., and Mann, S. C. "Problem Drinking in Hospitalized Schizophrenic Patients." *Addictive Behavior,* 1980, *5,* 273–276.

Alterman, A. I., Erdlen, F. R., and Murphy, E. "Alcohol Abuse in the Psychiatric Hospital Population." *Addictive Behavior,* 1981, *6,* 69–73.

Bachrach, L. L. "Young Adult Chronic Patients: An Analytical Review of the Literature." *Hospital and Community Psychiatry,* 1982, *33* (3), 189–197.

Bartels, S. J., Drake, R. E., Wallach, M. A. "Long-Term Course of Substance Use Disorders Among Patients with Severe Mental Illness." *Psychiatric Services,* 1995, *46,* 248–251.

Bartels, S. J., Drake, R. E., Wallach, M. A., and Freeman, D. H. "Characteristic Hostility in Schizophrenic Outpatients." *Schizophrenia Bulletin,* 1991, *17,* 163–171.

Bartels, S. J., Teague, G. B., Drake, R. E., Clark, R. E., Bush, P. W., and Noordsy, D. L. "Substance Abuse in Schizophrenia: Service Utilization and Costs." *Journal of Nervous and Mental Disease,* 1993, *181,* 227–232.

Bergman, H. C., and Harris, M. "Substance Abuse Among Young Adult Chronic Patients." *Psychosocial Rehabilitation Journal,* 1985, *9,* 49–54.

Brady, K., Anton, R., Ballenger, J. C., Lydiard, R. B., Adinoff, B., and Selander, J. "Cocaine Abuse Among Schizophrenic Patients." *American Journal of Psychiatry,* 1990, *147,* 1164–1167.

Buckley, P., Thompson, P., Way, L., and Meltzer, H. Y. "Substance Abuse Among Patients with Treatment-Resistant Schizophrenia: Characteristics and Implications for Clozapine Therapy." *American Journal of Psychiatry,* 1994, *151,* 385–391.

Cook, B. L., Winokur, G., and Fowler, R. C. "Classification of Alcoholism with Reference to Comorbidity." *Comprehensive Psychiatry,* 1994, *35,* 265–170.

Crum, R. M., Warner, L. A., Nelson, C. B., Schulenberg, J., Anthony, J. and Kessler, R. C. "Comorbidity of DSM-III-R Alcohol Abuse and Dependence with Other Psychiatric Disorders in The National Comorbidity Survey." Unpublished manuscript, 1995.

Cuffel, B. J. "Prevalence Estimates of Substance Abuse in Schizophrenia and Their Correlates." *Journal of Nervous and Mental Disease,* 1992, *180,* 589–592.

Cuffel, B. J., and Chase, P. "Remission and Relapse of Substance Use Disorder in Schizophrenia: Results from a One-Year Prospective Study." *Journal of Nervous and Mental Disease*, 1994, *182*, 342–348.

Cuffel, B. J., Heithoff, K. A., and Lawson, W. "Correlates of Patterns of Substance Abuse Among Patients with Schizophrenia." *Hospital and Community Psychiatry*, 1993, *44*, 247–251.

Cuffel, B. J., Shumway, M., Chouljian, T. L., and MacDonald, T. "A Longitudinal Study of Substance Use and Community Violence in Schizophrenia." *Journal of Nervous and Mental Disease*, 1994, *182*, 704–708.

Cuffel, B. J., Wait, D., and Head, T. "Shifting the Responsibility for State Hospital Services to Community Mental Health Agencies." *Hospital and Community Psychiatry*, 1994, *45*, 460–465.

Dixon, L., Haas, G., Weiden, P. J., Sweeney, J., and Frances, A. J. "Drug Abuse in Schizophrenic Patients: Clinical Correlates and Reasons for Use." *American Journal of Psychiatry*, 1991, *148*, 224–230.

Drake, R. E., Alterman, A. I., Rosenberg, S. R. "Detection of Substance Use Disorders in Severely Mentally Ill Patients." *Community Mental Health Journal*, 1993, *29*, 175–189.

Drake, R. E., McHugo, G. J., and Noordsy, D. L. "Treatment of Alcoholism Among Schizophrenic Outpatients: Four-Year Outcomes." *American Journal of Psychiatry*, 1993, *150*, 328–329.

Drake, R. E., Osher, F. C., and Wallach, M. A. "Alcohol Use and Abuse in Schizophrenia: A Prospective Community Study." *Journal of Nervous and Mental Disease*, 1989, *177*, 408–414.

Drake, R. E., and Wallach, M. A. "Substance Abuse Among the Chronically Mentally Ill." *Hospital and Community Psychiatry*, 1989, *40*, 1041–1046.

Drake, R. E., and Wallach, M. A. "Moderate Drinking Among People with Severe Mental Illness." *Hospital and Community Psychiatry*, 1993, *44*, 780–782.

Duke, P. J., Pantelis, C., and Barnes, T.R.E. "South Westminster Schizophrenia Survey: Alcohol Use and Its Relationship to Symptoms, Tardive Dyskinesia, and Illness Onset." *British Journal of Psychiatry*, 1994, *164*, 630–636.

Kessler, R. C., McGonagle, K. A., Zhao, S., Nelson, C. B., Hughes, M., Eshleman, S., Wittchen, H., and Kendler, K. S. "Lifetime and Twelve-Month Prevalence of DSM-III-R Psychiatric Disorders in the United States: Results from the National Comorbidity Survey." *Archives of General Psychiatry*, 1994, *51*, 8–19.

Kivlahan, D. R., Heiman, J. R., Wright, R. C., Mundt, J. W., and Shupe, J. A. "Treatment Cost and Rehospitalization Rate in Schizophrenic Outpatients with a History of Substance Abuse." *Hospital and Community Psychiatry*, 1991, *42*, 609–614.

Lehman, A. F., Myers, C. P., and Corty, E. "Assessment and Classification of Patients with Psychiatric and Substance Abuse Syndromes." *Hospital and Community Psychiatry*, 1989, *40*, 1019–1025.

Lehman, A. F., Myers, C. P., Corty, E., and Thompson, J. "Severity of Substance Use Disorders Among Psychiatric Inpatients." *Journal of Nervous and Mental Disease*, 1994, *182*, 164–167.

McCarrick, A. K., Manderscheid, R. W., and Bertolucci, D. E. "Correlates of Acting-Out Behaviors Among Young Adult Chronic Patients." *Hospital and Community Psychiatry*, 1985, *36* (8), 848–853.

Mueser, K. T., Bellack, A. S., and Blanchard, J. J. "Comorbidity of Schizophrenia and Substance Abuse: Implications for Treatment." *Journal of Consulting and Clinical Psychology*, 1992, *60*, 845–856.

Mueser, K. T., Bennett, M., and Kushner, M. G. "Epidemiology of Substance Use Disorders Among Persons with Chronic Mental Illnesses." In A. F. Lehman and L. Dixon (eds.), *Double Jeopardy: Chronic Mental Illnesses and Substance Abuse*. New York: Harwood Academic Publishers, 1995, 9–25.

Mueser, K. T., Yarnold, M. T., and Bellack, P. R. "Diagnostic and Demographic Correlates of Substance Abuse in Schizophrenia and Major Affective Disorder." *Acta Psychiatrica Scandanavica,* 1992, *85,* 48–55.

Mueser, K. T., Yarnold, P. R., Levinson, D. F., Singh, H., Bellack, A. S., Kee, K., Morrison, R. L., and Yadalam, K. G. "Prevalence of Substance Abuse in Schizophrenia: Demographic and Clinical Correlates." *Schizophrenia Bulletin,* 1990, *16,* 31–56.

Pepper, B., Kirshner, M. C., and Ryglewicz, H. "The Young Adult Chronic Patient: Overview of a Population." *Hospital and Community Psychiatry,* 1981, *32,* 463–469.

Regier, D. A., Farmer, M. E., Rae, D. S., Locke, B. Z., Keith, S. J., Judd, L. L., and Goodwin, F. K. "Comorbidity of Mental Disorders with Alcohol and Other Drug Abuse." *Journal of the American Medical Association,* 1990, *264,* 2511–2518.

Ries, R. K., and Ellingson, T. "A Pilot Assessment at One Month of Seventeen Dual Diagnosis Patients." *Hospital and Community Psychiatry,* 1990, *41,* 1230–1233.

Rosenthal, R. N., Hellerstein, D. J., and Miner, C. R. "Integrated Services for Treatment of Schizophrenic Substance Abusers: Demographics, Symptoms, and Substance Abuse Patterns." *Psychiatric Quarterly,* 1992, *63,* 3–26.

Schneier, F. R., and Siris, S. G. "A Review of Psychoactive Substance Use and Abuse in Schizophrenia: Patterns of Drug Choice." *Journal of Nervous and Mental Disease,* 1987, *175(11),* 641–652.

Sevy, S., Kay, S. R., Opler, L. A., and van Praag, H. M. "Significance of Cocaine History in Schizophrenia." *Journal of Nervous and Mental Disease,* 1990, *178,* 642–648.

Shaner, A., Khalsa, M. E., Roberts, L., Wilkins, J., Anglin, D., and Hsieh, S. "Unrecognized Cocaine Use Among Schizophrenic Patients." *American Journal of Psychiatry,* 1993, *150,* 758–762.

Shumway, M., Chouljian, T. L., and Hargreaves, W. A. "Patterns of Substance Use in Schizophrenia: A Markov Modeling Approach." *Journal of Psychiatric Research,* 1994, *28,* 277–287.

Shumway, M., and Cuffel, B.J. "Symptom Heterogeneity in Comorbid Alcohol Disorders," *Journal of Mental Health Administration,* in press.

Stone, A. M., Greenstein, R. A., Gamble, G., and McLellan, A. T. "Cocaine Use by Schizophrenic Outpatients Who Receive Depot Neuroleptic Medication." *Hospital and Community Psychiatry,* 1993, *44,* 176–177.

Test, M. A. "Training in Community Living." In R. P. Liberman (ed.), *Handbook of Psychiatric Rehabilitation.* New York: Macmillan, 1992, 153–170.

Tsuang, M. T., Simpson, J. C., and Kronfol, Z. "Subtypes of Drug Abuse with Psychosis." *Archives of General Psychiatry,* 1982, *39,* 141–147.

Turner, W. M., and Tsuang, M. T. "Impact of Substance Abuse on the Course and Outcome of Schizophrenia." *Schizophrenia Bulletin,* 1990, *16,* 87–95.

Weiss, R. D., Mirin, S. M., and Frances, R. J. "The Myth of the Typical Dual Diagnosis Patient." *Hospital and Community Psychiatry,* 1992, *43,* 107–108.

BRIAN J. CUFFEL, Ph.D., is adjunct assistant professor in the Department of Psychology at Santa Clara University and in the Department of Psychiatry at the University of California, San Francisco.

# CONCLUSION

The contributions to this volume provide ample evidence that important steps have been made in recent years towards understanding how to improve services for dually diagnosed persons. The progress made over such a brief period of time has made this field an exciting, dynamic area for clinicians, service administrators, and researchers alike, and the landscape is likely to continue to change in the future. In this concluding section, we highlight some of the advances made, and point to new directions in need of investigation.

The chapter by Drake, Rosenberg, and Mueser shows that steady progress has been made in the refinement of strategies for the assessment of substance use disorders in persons with severe psychiatric illnesses. Substance abuse has different presentations, correlates, and clinical implications among dually diagnosed individuals, as compared with the general population. Until new instruments are developed, existing ones must be adapted and combined to maximize the utility of assessment. Furthermore, the importance of multimodal assessments that take into account clinicians' observations as well as client reports, observations from significant others, and biological assays, is now more fully appreciated. We anticipate that new instruments for screening and diagnostic assessment will be more sensitive and specific for this population.

The chapters by Carey on treatment guidelines and by Mueser and Noordsy on group treatment summarize the continuing evolution of intervention models for dually diagnosed clients. Carey presents guidelines for treating severe mental illness and substance abuse that incorporate both motivational and behavioral strategies into a cohesive framework. Mueser and Noordsy describe four different group models (twelve-step, educational-supportive, social skill, and stagewise), and summarize the research supporting the different models. Both chapters illustrate how research can be incorporated into current clinical programming. At this point, research indicates that integrated dual-diagnosis treatment is more effective than parallel treatment, but specific aspects of treatment, many of which are discussed in these two chapters, require empirical validation. As new findings emerge over the next few years, clinical guidelines will become more precise.

The chapters by Osher and Dixon on housing and by Clark on families represent relatively new forays into exploring the impact of substance abuse in these clients. Problems maintaining stable housing for the dually diagnosed have gained in prominence as the population of homeless persons has grown. As Osher and Dixon point out, the failure to provide safe housing alternatives places clients at risk for continued substance abuse and its attendant consequences.

New approaches to meeting the housing needs of these persons must be considered. Clark reviews evidence that poor family relationships, or the absence of contact with relatives, may contribute to homelessness. Family work holds multiple promises, including improving the quality of lives of both relatives and clients, reducing substance abuse, and staving off burnout leading to homelessness. Research in both areas will be essential in identifying effective approaches.

Jerrell's chapter addresses the critical question of how to improve substance abuse in the most cost-effective manner by illustrating one approach to the problem in a recently completed study. Ultimately, of course, all clinical interventions must be justified, at least partly, on the basis of cost-effectiveness and cost-benefit analyses. As this question has been examined in so few studies of interventions for dually diagnosed persons, Jerrell's efforts are pioneering. Future research will need to be considered in light of her work.

Cuffel's chapter summarizes the literature on the high prevalence of substance use disorders among the severely mentally ill and reviews intriguing longitudinal data suggesting that recovery from substance abuse results in improved clinical and functional outcomes. These findings provide strong encouragement that efforts to treat substance abuse in this population will translate into meaningful changes in the lives of these clients.

Much progress has been made. But in many ways this progress has accentuated the gaps in our understanding of how to best meet the needs of this challenging population. Some examples of these gaps follow. We know the limits of our existing instruments for assessing substance abuse in these clients, but satisfactory (i.e., reliable, valid, cost-effective) instruments await development at this time. Several clinical models have been articulated but long-term outcomes need to be studied. The problems of housing and family burden are better understood than before but strategies for improving these domains have not yet been formally evaluated. Cost-effectiveness analysis in this area is still in its infancy and is likely to be a complex issue in this era of changing fiscal policies, priorities, and funding structures. The epidemiological evidence showing high rates of substance use disorder among the severely mentally ill is overwhelming, yet the prevention of substance abuse in these clients has not been addressed. Similarly, researchers have only begun to study the clinical implications of heterogeneity among clients with dual disorders.

Advances in both science and mental health services often occur in dramatic fashion. The fact that we are now faced with more questions than ever before is not a sign that we are going backwards; it is a sign of progress, because we are learning which questions need to be asked. We are confident that continued effort will result in even more changes and better outcomes for persons with severe mental illness and substance abuse.

## Additional Resources

For those who are interested in further reading, a list of available publications on the assessment and treatment of dually diagnosed persons can be obtained from either of the editors at the following address: New Hampshire–Dartmouth Psychiatric Research Center, Main Building, 105 Pleasant St., Concord, N.H., 03301.

In addition, we recommend another recently published book that summarizes advances in dual diagnosis:

Lehman, A., and Dixon, L. (eds.). *Double Jeopardy: Chronic Mental Illness and Substance Abuse.* New York: Harwood Academic Publishers, 1995.

Robert E. Drake
Kim T. Mueser
Editors

# Name Index

111

# Subject Index

Abstinence approach, 25–27
Active treatment groups, 38–39
Alcoholics Anonymous (AA), 27, 33–35, 81–82
Assertive community teams (ACTs), 53–54
Assessment, substance abuse: abuse duration and, 11; associated conditions and, 11–12; behavioral factors and, 10; cognitive factors and, 10; complicating factors and, 4; detection and, 4–8; environmental factors and, 10; functions of, 4; future research on, 12–13; lack of standardized measure for, 10; nondetection and, 4–5; patient change sequence and, 11; physiological factors and, 10; specialized, 4, 10–12; structured interviews and, 6; substance-using behaviors and, 10–11; symptom severity and, 11; treatment stage and, 11. *See also* Substance abuse

Behavioral skills training model, 81

Case management model, 81
Collateral sources, 7
Comorbid substance use disorder: debate about, 94; DSM-III-R groupings of, 96; Epidemiologic Catchment Area study of, 94; future research on, 102; gaps in knowledge of, 108; gender and, 97, 99; health care costs of, 103; large-scale community surveys on, 94; literature review of, 94–95; misunderstanding of, 93; multiple substance use and, 98; National Comorbidity Study and, 94; negative life consequences of, 102; population characteristics and, 99; predicting, 103; prevalence of, 5, 94–96; prevention/intervention programs and, 102–103; Program for Assertive Community Treatment teams and, 101; relapse rates and, 99–101; remission rates and, 100–101; schizophrenia and, 94–95, 98–99, 102; severity of, 98; substance abuse patterns and, 96–98; substance abuse prevalence and, 94–96; substance-symptom connection and,

95–96; symptom interaction and, 93; usage rates and, 100; violent behavior and, 97–98. *See also* Dually diagnosed persons; Substance use disorder
Continuum (level-of-care) housing model, 50
Co-occurring disorders. *See* Comorbid substance use disorder; Dually diagnosed persons
Coping skills training, 28. *See also* Social skills training (SST)
Cost-effective treatment, dual diagnosis (study): behavioral skills training model and, 81–82, 84–86, 89–90; case management model and, 81–82, 84–86, 89–90; findings, 84–89; further research, 89–90; implications, 89–90; limitations, 90; methods, 83–84; program implementation, 81–83; purpose, 80; setting, 80–81; twelve-step program model and, 81–82, 84–86, 89

Damp housing, 60
Detection, substance abuse: collateral sources and, 7; index of suspicion and, 6; interview instruments for, 6–7; laboratory tests and, 7–8; multiple methods for, 5–6; other procedures for, 8; self-reports and, 6–7. *See also* Substance abuse
Diagnosis, substance abuse: complicating factors and, 8; criteria, 8; as DSM category, 8–9; heterogeneity and, 10; treatment considerations and, 10. *See also* Substance abuse
Double Trouble groups, 27
Dry housing, 60
Dually diagnosed persons: abstinence and, 25; barriers to services for, 55–56; case examples, 3–4, 19–20, 65–66; clinical issues and, 56–57; coercive approaches with, 59; continuum of care and, 27–28; criminal behavior of, 56, 79, 97–98; crisis intervention for, 58; daily living difficulties of, 66; denial of, 58; discrimination against, 55–56; effective interdependence of, 75; eviction of, 56–57; health care reform and, 55;

# Ordering Information

NEW DIRECTIONS FOR MENTAL HEALTH SERVICES is a series of paperback books that presents timely and readable volumes on subjects of concern to clinicians, administrators, and others involved in the care of the mentally disabled. Each volume is devoted to one topic and includes a broad range of authoritative articles written by noted specialists in the field. Books in the series are published quarterly in Spring, Summer, Fall, and Winter and are available for purchase by subscription as well as individually.

SUBSCRIPTIONS for 1996 cost $59.00 for individuals (a savings of 22 percent over single-copy prices) and $87.00 for institutions, agencies, and libraries. Standing orders are accepted. New York residents, add local sales tax for subscriptions. (For subscriptions outside the United States, add $7.00 for shipping via surface mail or $25.00 for air mail. Orders *must be prepaid* in U.S. dollars by check drawn on a U.S. bank or charged to VISA, MasterCard, or American Express.)

SINGLE COPIES cost $19.00 plus shipping (see below) when payment accompanies order. California, New Jersey, New York, and Washington, D.C., residents, please include appropriate sales tax. Canadian residents, add GST and any local taxes. Billed orders will be charged shipping and handling. No billed shipments to post office boxes. (Orders from outside the United States *must be prepaid* by check drawn on a U.S. bank or charged to VISA, MasterCard, or American Express.)

SHIPPING (SINGLE COPIES ONLY): one issue, add $5.00; two issues, add $6.00; three issues, add $7.00; four to five issues, add $8.00; six to seven issues, add $9.00; eight or more issues, add $12.00.

DISCOUNTS FOR QUANTITY ORDERS are available. Please write to the address below for information.

ALL ORDERS must include either the name of an individual or an official purchase order number. Please submit your order as follows:
   *Subscriptions:* specify series and year subscription is to begin
   *Single copies:* include individual title code (such as MHS59)

MAIL ALL ORDERS TO:
   Jossey-Bass Publishers
   350 Sansome Street
   San Francisco, California 94104-1342

FOR SUBSCRIPTION SALES OUTSIDE OF THE UNITED STATES, contact any international subscription agency or Jossey-Bass directly.